the Cook's Canvas 2

Coastal Carolina Artfully Entertains

CAMERON ART MUSEUM

Wilmington, North Carolina

the Cook's Canvas₂

Coastal Carolina Artfully Entertains

Published by Louise Wells Cameron Art Museum

Louise Wells Cameron Art Museum
3201 South 17th Street
Wilmington, North Carolina 28412
910.395.5999
www.cameronartmuseum.com
www.CooksCanvas.com

COVER ART AND ENDSHEET: *Beach Cottage*, 1981 by Claude Howell (American, 1915–1997), oil on canvas. Gift of the friends of Claude Howell © Claude Howell Estate/Cameron Art Museum. Photograph © 2007 by Cameron Art Museum.

Page 272 constitutes an extension of this copyright page.

This cookbook is a collection of favorite recipes, which are not necessarily original recipes.

ISBN: 978-0-9793359-1-4

Edited, Designed, and Manufactured by

FRP

P. O. Box 305142
Nashville, Tennessee 37230
800-358-0560

Printed in China
First Printing: 2007
5,000 copies

Note: All recipes have been tested using large eggs, unsalted butter, and the freshest ingredients available, including freshly grated or shredded cheeses and seasonings. Differences in flavor and texture may result from using other products.

Dedication

Since its beginning, our Museum has been fortunate to have a multitude of volunteers who have enabled the Museum to educate and enchant the public with fine art, crafts and design, and innovative programming.

The Cook's Canvas 2: Coastal Carolina Artfully Entertains is dedicated with gratitude to our tireless volunteers who gave their time, talents, and enthusiasm in making the Museum what it is today and by making both editions of *The Cook's Canvas* possible.

Our volunteers are our foundation, our fortitude, and our future. They have all contributed to the Cameron Art Museum's quest to be a premier cultural destination in North Carolina.

Thank you, volunteers!

Contents

Preface

The Cook's Canvas 2: Coastal Carolina Artfully Entertains celebrates our coastal lifestyle and the art of entertaining. Whether you are an expert or a novice, this is a cookbook with recipes for every occasion, from a simple weekday dinner with the family to an elegant dinner party. The recipes may be easy or complicated, but each reflects a dish that one would be proud to serve.

The recipes in our cookbook were collected from more than two hundred Wilmington cooks as well as from friends around the country with Wilmington connections. Each recipe was tested by volunteers at tasting parties and then selected. The more than 260 recipes are easy to follow, and the results are distinctive and unique. They will create new favorite dishes for your family and friends. We hope you will try each one!

The Cook's Canvas was published in 1996 to benefit the then St. John's Museum of Art in Wilmington, North Carolina. The cookbook was self-published, self-marketed, and sold out. In 2002, the Museum moved to a larger, state-of-the-art facility and was renamed the Cameron Art Museum. As there had been many requests for another cookbook, we began to compile *The Cook's Canvas 2: Coastal Carolina Artfully Entertains*.

This cookbook reminds us of the importance of sitting at a dinner table, laughing with friends and family, and enjoying the moment. Eating should be an experience to share with your family, a special someone in your life, or a gathering of friends, formal or informal.

Creative and enthusiastic volunteers of the Cameron Art Museum have contributed to making this cookbook a must-have for your kitchen shelf. We are certain that you will enjoy artfully entertaining your family and friends with our recipes.

The Executive Committee
The Cook's Canvas 2: Coastal Carolina Artfully Entertains

Proceeds from the sale of *The Cook's Canvas 2: Coastal Carolina Artfully Entertains* will benefit the children's programs at the Cameron Art Museum, Wilmington, North Carolina.

Committee Members

Executive Committee

Mary Coble

Hilda Dill

Robin Hackney

Anne Livingston

Ann Robins

Dixey Smith

Other Committee Members

Andrea Tetrick, Secretary

Betsy Bede, Editor

Ann Skiba, Editor

Diana Corbett, Treasurer

Rick Myracle, Marketing

Peggy Pancoe Rosoff, Marketing

Liz Coffey, Graphic Design

Jackie Margoles, Public Relations

Ben Parsley, Web Site

Kemille Moore, Art

Margie Worthington, Art

Suzanne Coleman, Consultant

Hilda Godwin, Consultant

Sarah Lowe, Consultant

Foreword

The Cameron Art Museum exists today as a testament to the generosity of its patrons, supporters, and volunteers. Countless individuals have worked to build and sustain this Museum, and this book represents another such act of generosity and support for the only art museum in southeastern North Carolina. This project, *The Cook's Canvas 2,* was conceived as a vehicle to raise funds for the Museum's family and children's programs. Each month the museum hosts "Kids at CAM," a family event featuring quality art activities relating to the Museum's current exhibitions. A central feature of this monthly event includes child docents who provide tours through the current exhibitions for other children and their families. Our young docents have remained one of the most popular aspects of these monthly Kids at CAM events.

We wish to extend our deepest thanks to the many volunteers of the Cookbook Committee who both conceived the cookbook and developed the recipes contained herein. Special thanks are due the members of the Executive Committee, without whom this cookbook project would not be possible. We are so grateful to Mary Coble, Hilda Dill, Robin Hackney, Anne Livingston, Ann Robins, and Dixey Smith for their diligent and creative efforts. Our appreciation also goes to the many volunteers on the committee who shared their time, financial support . . . and recipes! We are also grateful to the many individuals and businesses who underwrote this project, ensuring that every dollar raised through the sale of these books will directly support the Museum's children's and family programming.

We are proud of this community's commitment to enable The Cameron Art Museum to fulfill its mission, bringing beautiful and enlightening art experiences to visitors of all ages. Our efforts to engage, enchant, and transform human lives through our exhibitions and programs would not be possible without the help of supporters and patrons like the volunteers comprising the Cookbook Committee.

We hope this cookbook brings you many happy and delicious moments.

Deborah Velders
Director

Silver Service Sponsors

Dan Cameron Family Foundation

Lelia P. Birrell

Diana & Scott Corbett

Hilda & Matthew Dill

Dixey & Dick Smith

Signature Homes of Wilmington

Robin & Deans Hackney

Mary Clifford & Bill Boyd

Cyndi & Ronnie McNeill

Bald Head Island Construction

Betty H. Cameron

Mary & John Coble

Charlotte Anne Cameron

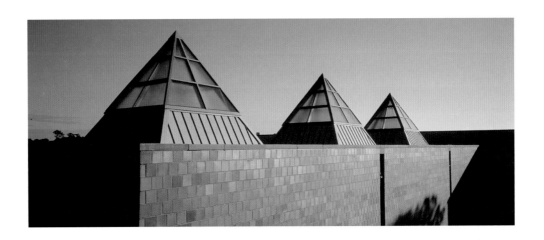

Gwathmey Siegel & Associates Architects llc
New York, NY
Detail of Cameron Art Museum
Photograph by Brownie Harris

Appetizers

The Cook's Canvas 2

Sesame Beef Strips

1¹/2 pounds flank steak or London broil
3/4   cup olive oil
2/3   cup packed brown sugar
2/3   cup soy sauce
2/3   cup dry sherry
2/3   cup pineapple juice (optional)
1/2   cup toasted sesame oil
2   garlic cloves, minced
1   teaspoon minced fresh ginger
      Bamboo skewers

- Cut the beef into paper-thin slices across the grain.
- Combine the olive oil, brown sugar, soy sauce, sherry, pineapple juice, sesame oil, garlic and ginger in a bowl; mix well.
- Add the beef to the marinade and toss until coated. Marinate, covered, in the refrigerator for 2 to 10 hours.
- Thread the beef onto skewers that have been soaked in water for 15 minutes and place on a rack in a broiler pan. Brush the beef heavily with the marinade.
- Broil on High for 90 seconds.
- Remove from the heat and turn the beef over. Brush the beef heavily with the marinade, discarding any remaining marinade.
- Broil until the beef reaches the desired degree of doneness. Serve hot or at room temperature.
- For an entrée, broil the beef strips in a baking pan without threading on skewers and serve with a salad. As an alternative, marinate and cook the flank steak or London broil whole. Slice the cooked beef and serve it over mixed salad greens with a vinaigrette.

Serves 8

Note: The longer the beef marinates, the more flavor it will have. Soaking the skewers prevents them from burning. For ready-to-use skewers, freeze soaked skewers and use them directly from the freezer.

Veal Meatballs with Caper Mayonnaise

3   (3/4-inch-thick) slices stale
    Italian bread
2/3 pound ground veal
3   sweet Italian sausages, casings
    removed (about 12 ounces)
2   eggs, lightly beaten
1/4 cup freshly grated
    Parmesan cheese
3   tablespoons minced
    fresh parsley

1/2 teaspoon salt
1/4 teaspoon freshly
    grated nutmeg
    Freshly ground pepper to taste
1   cup very fine stale white
    bread crumbs
    Olive oil or peanut oil
    Caper Mayonnaise (below)

■ Moisten the bread slices with water or milk and squeeze dry. Process the moistened
  bread, veal, sausages, eggs, cheese, parsley, salt, nutmeg and pepper in a food
  processor, pulsing until well combined. Chill, covered, for 1 hour.

■ Shape the veal mixture into 1-inch balls and roll in the bread crumbs, coating well.
  Cook the meatballs in batches in olive oil in a skillet for 5 minutes or until cooked
  through and evenly brown. Drain on paper towels. Arrange the meatballs on a
  serving platter and serve with Caper Mayonnaise.

Makes 5 dozen

Caper Mayonnaise

2   egg yolks, at room temperature
1   tablespoon fresh lemon juice
1 1/2 cups olive oil
2   tablespoons drained capers

1   or 2 tablespoons
    anchovy paste
    Salt and freshly ground
    pepper to taste

■ Combine the egg yolks, lemon juice and 3 tablespoons of the olive oil in a food
  processor. Pulse until the mixture thickens slightly.

■ Add the remaining olive oil in a fine stream, processing constantly until smooth and
  thick. Spoon into a small bowl and fold in the anchovy paste and capers. Season with
  salt and pepper and chill until serving time.

Makes 1 3/4 cups

*Note: If you are concerned about using raw egg yolks, use yolks from eggs pasteurized in
their shells, which are sold at some specialty food stores, or use an equivalent amount of
pasteurized egg substitute.*

BLT New Potatoes

2	pounds small new potatoes	1	cup mayonnaise
	Salt and freshly ground	1	pound bacon, crisp-cooked
	pepper to taste		and crumbled
1	cup sour cream	1	tomato, chopped

- Cut the potatoes into halves. Trim the opposite sides and lay the potatoes, flat center side up, on a greased baking sheet. Season with salt and pepper.
- Bake, covered with aluminum foil, for 1 hour or until tender. Let stand until cool.
- Scoop out and discard a small portion of the center of the potato halves with a small melon baller; chill, covered, until serving time.
- Combine the sour cream and mayonnaise in a bowl and blend until smooth. Stir in the bacon and tomato. Season with pepper.
- Spoon the sour cream mixture into the potatoes and place flat on a serving tray.

Serves 15

Note: This filling is also great piped into cherry tomatoes or served as a dip with potato chips. Store in the refrigerator.

Ham and Okra Roll-Ups

8	ounces Herb Cheese Spread (*page 31*), softened	1	(12-ounce) package sliced rectangular ham, patted dry
1	tablespoon dried minced onion	1	(16-ounce) jar pickled okra, drained and stems removed
1	teaspoon seasoned salt		

- Combine the cheese, onion and seasoned salt in a bowl and mix well.
- Spread the cheese mixture evenly over the ham slices. Place 1 or 2 okra pods lengthwise at one side of each of the ham slices and roll tightly.
- Chill, covered, until firm. Slice horizontally.

Serves 8

Variation: Substitute pickled asparagus for the okra.

Savory Lettuce Wraps

2 slices fresh ginger, minced
1/4 cup peanut oil
4 ounces bamboo shoots, chopped
4 water chestnuts, chopped
2 garlic cloves, minced
1 pound lean ground pork
1 scallion, chopped
1 teaspoon salt
1/4 teaspoon freshly ground pepper
1 tablespoon light soy sauce
1 tablespoon dry sherry
1/2 tablespoon hoisin sauce
1 1/2 teaspoons sugar
1 1/2 teaspoons toasted sesame oil
12 iceberg lettuce leaves
   Hoisin sauce

- Sauté the ginger in the hot peanut oil in a wok for 30 seconds.
- Add the bamboo shoots, water chestnuts and garlic and stir-fry for 1 minute.
- Add the pork, scallion, salt and pepper and stir-fry for 2 minutes or until the pork is cooked through.
- Add the soy sauce, sherry, hoisin sauce and sugar and stir-fry for 3 minutes.
- Add the sesame oil and toss until well incorporated. Remove from the heat.
- Spoon the pork mixture onto each lettuce leaf. Top with hoisin sauce and roll as for an egg roll. Serve immediately.

Makes 12

Note: *It is fun to have your guests roll their own lettuce wraps. Spoon the pork mixture into a serving bowl and place on a serving platter that is larger than the bowl. Arrange the lettuce leaves around the bowl. Serve hoisin sauce on the side.*

Down South Pork and Sage Handpies

1   small onion, minced
3   tablespoons butter
1   pound lean ground pork
1   potato, boiled, peeled and cut into cubes
1   baking apple, peeled and chopped
1¹/₂ tablespoons all-purpose flour
2   tablespoons rubbed sage
1   tablespoon dark brown sugar
¹/₄ teaspoon salt
¹/₂ teaspoon freshly ground pepper
     Pie pastry, chilled
     Egg yolks, lightly beaten

- Sauté the onion in the butter in a skillet for 5 minutes.
- Add the pork and cook for 10 minutes, stirring until brown and crumbly.
- Add the potato, apple and flour and cook for 2 minutes, stirring frequently.
- Stir in the sage, brown sugar, salt and pepper and remove from the heat.
- Roll the pastry to ¹/₈ inch thick. Cut with a 2¹/₂-inch biscuit cutter. Use half the pastry at a time, keeping the remaining pastry well chilled.
- Spoon a heaping teaspoon of the pork mixture in the center of each of the pastry rounds. Brush the edge of the pastry rounds lightly with water. Fold the pastry over filling to make half circles. Press the edges lightly with a fork to seal and crimp.
- Brush the tops with egg yolk and place on a baking sheet.
- Bake at 400 degrees for 20 to 30 minutes or until golden brown. Serve warm or at room temperature.
- May be made ahead of time and chilled or frozen, covered, until ready to bake.

Makes 3 dozen

Note: *Handpies were originally portable lunches for farmers to take to the fields. Bring to room temperature before baking. These pies may also be filled with mashed potatoes mixed with goat cheese, caramelized onion, salt and pepper.*

Jalapeño Corn Bread Bites

2 cups self-rising buttermilk corn bread mix
1¹/2 cups buttermilk
¹/4 cup vegetable oil
1 egg
¹/2 cup finely chopped jalapeño chile, or to taste
Tarragon Butter (*below*) or tarragon mayonnaise
8 ounces thinly sliced smoked turkey or country ham

- Combine the corn bread mix, buttermilk, oil, egg and jalapeño chile in a bowl and mix well.
- Fill lightly greased miniature muffin tins ²/3 full.
- Bake at 400 degrees for 10 to 15 minutes or until light golden brown. Let stand until cool enough to handle.
- Slice the muffins three-fourths of the way through. Spread the inside with the Tarragon Butter and fill with a slice of the turkey or country ham. Serve warm.

Makes 3 dozen

Note: *This appetizer may be assembled ahead of time and frozen. Reheat to serve.*

Tarragon Butter

1 cup (2 sticks) butter, softened
1 tablespoon dried tarragon
1 tablespoon dried minced onion

- Combine the butter, tarragon and onion in a bowl and mix until well combined.
- Store in the refrigerator.

Makes 1 cup

Shrimp Endive

1   pound cooked shrimp, peeled and deveined
8   ounces cream cheese, softened
1/4 cup mayonnaise
     Salt and freshly ground pepper to taste
4   small shallots, minced
2   tablespoons drained and rinsed capers
     Belgian endive leaves
     Cooked shrimp, split, or alfalfa sprouts (optional)
     Paprika

- Pulse the shrimp in a food processor with a steel blade until finely chopped.
- Add the cream cheese, mayonnaise, salt and pepper and pulse just until blended. Do not overprocess.
- Spoon the shrimp mixture into a small bowl and stir in the shallots and capers.
- Pipe the shrimp mixture with a wide nozzle into the base of the endive leaves and arrange on a serving platter. Chill, covered, until serving time. Garnish with split shrimp or alfalfa sprouts. Sprinkle with paprika.

Serves 8

Variation: *Spoon the shrimp mixture into a small terrine, mold or bowl lined with plastic wrap. Chill, covered, until firm and unmold onto a serving platter. Sprinkle with paprika and serve with crackers and endive leaves. When endive is unavailable, serve on or with sliced cucumber rounds.*

Confetti Shrimp

1 1/2 pounds large shrimp, peeled and deveined
2 tablespoons olive oil
3 tablespoons minced fresh ginger (about 1 1/4 ounces)
2 garlic cloves, minced
1 1/2 tablespoons fresh lemon juice
1 tablespoon fresh lime juice
1/4 teaspoon salt
2 tablespoons olive oil
1/2 teaspoon Chinese hot red chili oil
1 (4-ounce) jar roasted red bell pepper, drained and minced
1/4 cup minced fresh chives or scallions (green part only)

- Sauté the shrimp in 2 tablespoons olive oil in a skillet over high heat for 2 to 3 minutes or until the shrimp turn pink.
- Remove the shrimp to a bowl and let stand until cool, reserving the pan drippings in the skillet.
- Reduce the heat to low. Sauté the ginger and garlic in the pan drippings in the skillet for 3 minutes or until tender. Spoon with pan drippings into a bowl.
- Add the lemon juice, lime juice and salt to the ginger mixture and whisk well.
- Add 2 tablespoons olive oil and the hot red chili oil and whisk until the oils are blended.
- Pour the marinade over the shrimp and toss until coated. Let stand at room temperature for 1 hour.
- Drain the shrimp, discarding the marinade, and fold in the roasted bell pepper and chives.
- Spoon the shrimp mixture into a serving bowl and serve with cocktail picks.

Serves 6

Note: To roast peppers, broil bell peppers on a baking sheet on the highest rack on High for 5 minutes or until the skin is completely blistered and charred black, turning often. Place the peppers in a small paper bag and fold the top of the bag over, securing well. Let stand for 10 minutes. Remove the bell peppers from the bag and remove the charred skin, stem and seeds.

New Orleans Shrimp

2 quarts water
1/2 cup sliced onion
2 ribs celery with leaves
1 garlic clove, peeled
1 bay leaf
1 1/2 teaspoons salt

1/8 teaspoon cayenne pepper
2 pounds shrimp
1/2 lemon, sliced
New Orleans Shrimp Sauce
(below)

- Combine the water, onion, celery, garlic, bay leaf, salt and cayenne pepper in a large saucepan. Bring to a simmer and cook for 15 minutes.
- Add the shrimp and lemon and cook until the shrimp turn pink. Drain, discarding the liquid. Let stand until cool. Peel the shrimp.
- Place the shrimp in a serving bowl and add the sauce, tossing until coated.
- Marinate, covered, in the refrigerator for up to 12 hours. Serve in the New Orleans Shrimp Sauce with cocktail picks.

Serves 8

New Orleans Shrimp Sauce

1 garlic clove, cut into halves
1 scallion, finely chopped
1/2 cup finely chopped celery
6 tablespoons olive oil
3 tablespoons lemon juice
2 tablespoons chili sauce
2 tablespoons ketchup
2 tablespoons horseradish

1 tablespoon mustard
1 tablespoon finely chopped chives
1/2 teaspoon hot red pepper sauce
1/2 teaspoon paprika
3/4 teaspoon salt

- Rub a bowl with the cut sides of the garlic; discard garlic.
- Add the scallion, celery, olive oil, lemon juice, chili sauce, ketchup, horseradish, mustard, chives, hot sauce, paprika and salt; mix well.

Makes 1 1/2 cups

Variation: This sauce is also great served with crab claws.

Grilled Citrus Shrimp with Summer Basil Dipping Sauce

1 1/2 teaspoons grated orange zest
1/2 cup fresh orange juice
1 1/2 teaspoons grated lime zest
1/4 cup fresh lime juice
1 small shallot, minced
1 garlic clove, minced
Leaves of 2 to 3 fresh thyme sprigs, chopped
1 teaspoon sherry vinegar

1/4 teaspoon kosher salt
1/8 teaspoon freshly ground pepper
1/4 cup olive oil
1 pound large shrimp, peeled and deveined
Summer Basil Dipping Sauce (*below*)
Skewers

- Combine the orange zest, orange juice, lime zest, lime juice, shallot, garlic, thyme, vinegar, salt and pepper in a bowl; whisk well.
- Add the olive oil gradually, whisking constantly until incorporated.
- Add the shrimp and toss until coated. Marinate for 30 minutes. Drain, discarding the marinade.
- Thread the shrimp onto skewers or place in a grill basket. Grill for 2 to 3 minutes on each side or until the shrimp turn pink. Serve with the Summer Basil Dipping Sauce.

Serves 4

Summer Basil Dipping Sauce

3 cups fresh basil leaves
1/4 cup red wine vinegar
3 anchovy fillets, chopped
1 tablespoon Dijon mustard

3/4 teaspoon kosher salt
3/4 cup extra-virgin olive oil
1/2 teaspoon freshly ground pepper

- Process the basil, vinegar, anchovy, Dijon mustard and salt in a food processor with a steel blade for 30 seconds.
- Add the olive oil gradually, processing constantly until combined. Season with the pepper. Store in the refrigerator.

Makes 1 1/2 cups

Note: *May be stored in a container with a tight-fitting lid for up to two weeks.*

Crab Canapés

1   pound crab meat (*see Note*)
1/4 cup tarragon vinegar
1/3 cup mayonnaise
3   tablespoons chopped drained pimento
2   tablespoons minced green onion
1   tablespoon drained capers
1   teaspoon salt
1/2 teaspoon freshly ground pepper
      Crackers or crostini

- Combine the crab meat and vinegar in a bowl and toss gently to combine. Marinate, covered, in the refrigerator for at least 30 minutes or up to 3 hours. Drain, discarding the liquid.
- Fold in the mayonnaise, pimento, green onion, capers, salt and pepper.
- Spoon the crab meat mixture onto crackers or crostini.

Serves 8

Note: To clean crab meat, carefully pick through the crab meat and remove any pieces of cartilage or shells. Do not rinse with water.

Poached Salmon with Lemon Cucumber Sauce

4   cups water
1/2 cup white wine
1   small onion, cut into quarters and sliced lengthwise
10 peppercorns
1   teaspoon salt

4   (6-ounce) salmon fillets or steaks
    Lemon Cucumber Sauce (*below*)
    Melba toast

- Combine the water, wine, onion, peppercorns and salt in a large deep skillet. Bring to a boil.
- Add the salmon and return to a boil. Lower the heat and simmer for 10 minutes or until the salmon begins to flake easily when tested with a fork. Remove salmon with a slotted spoon to cutting board.
- Flake the fish and arrange on a serving platter. Serve with melba toast and the Lemon Cucumber Sauce on the side.

Serves 12

Lemon Cucumber Sauce

1   large cucumber, peeled, seeded and chopped
1/4 cup mayonnaise
1/4 cup sour cream

1   teaspoon grated lemon zest
1   teaspoon lemon juice
1   teaspoon minced onion
    Salt to taste

- Combine the cucumber, mayonnaise, sour cream, lemon zest, lemon juice and onion in a bowl; mix well. Season with salt.
- Chill, covered, until serving time.

Makes 1 1/2 cups

Variation: *To serve as an entrée for a seated dinner party of four, pair the salmon with Pesto Rice Timbales (page 191).*

Capered Deviled Eggs

8   eggs
1/2   cup mayonnaise
1   tablespoon Dijon mustard
1/4   cup crisp-cooked and crumbled bacon
1   small shallot, finely chopped
1   tablespoon drained capers
1   teaspoon chopped parsley
1/2   teaspoon grated lemon zest
1/2   teaspoon garlic powder
    Salt and freshly ground pepper to taste
    Paprika

- Place the eggs in a saucepan and cover with cold water. Bring to a boil.
- Cover with a lid and turn off the heat. Let stand for 15 minutes.
- Drain, discarding the water. Place the eggs in an ice water bath until cool.
- Peel and cut the eggs into halves lengthwise. Remove the yolks and mash with a fork in a bowl.
- Add the mayonnaise and Dijon mustard and blend until smooth.
- Fold in the bacon, shallot, capers, parsley, lemon zest and garlic powder. Season with salt and pepper.
- Fill each egg white half with a heaping mound of the yolk mixture.
- Chill until serving time. Sprinkle with paprika just before serving.

Makes 16

Note: *This also makes wonderful egg salad.*

Wild Mushroom and Goat Cheese Pastries

2	shallots, minced
1	garlic clove, minced
1	tablespoon butter
1	pound shiitake mushrooms or other wild mushrooms, finely chopped
1	(8-count) can refrigerator crescent rolls, separated
4	ounces cream cheese, softened
4	ounces goat cheese, softened
2	tablespoons minced drained oil-pack sun-dried tomatoes
1	teaspoon thyme
1	egg, lightly beaten

- Sauté the shallots and garlic in the butter until translucent.
- Add the mushrooms and sauté for 5 minutes or until tender. Let stand until cool.
- Cut each crescent roll into 2 smaller triangles.
- Combine the cream cheese and goat cheese in a bowl and blend until smooth.
- Fold in the mushroom mixture, sun-dried tomatoes and thyme.
- Spoon 1 tablespoon of the cheese mixture in the center of each of the crescent roll halves.
- Fold one edge of the triangle over the filling and press the edges together, sealing in the filling. Brush with the egg.
- Bake on a greased baking sheet for 10 minutes or until brown. Serve immediately.

Serves 8

Note: *May make these pastries ahead and freeze until ready to bake.*

Cheese Wafers with Candied Ginger

2¼ cups (9 ounces) grated sharp Cheddar cheese
1 cup (2 sticks) butter, softened
2 cups all-purpose flour
1 teaspoon salt
2 teaspoons red pepper, or to taste
2 cups crisp rice cereal
Candied ginger

- Combine the cheese and butter in a bowl and mix until blended.
- Add the flour, salt and red pepper and mix well.
- Fold in the cereal carefully. Do not crush the cereal.
- Drop the dough by teaspoonfuls onto a baking sheet. Flatten each with the back of a fork and press a piece of candied ginger into the center.
- Bake at 350 degrees for 10 minutes.

Makes 4 dozen

Spicy Hot Almonds

1 pound whole almonds
2 tablespoons olive oil
1 tablespoon Worcestershire sauce
1 teaspoon cumin
1 teaspoon garlic powder
1 teaspoon salt
1 teaspoon cayenne pepper

- Combine the almonds, olive oil, Worcestershire sauce, cumin, garlic powder, salt and cayenne pepper in a sealable plastic bag. Shake until the almonds are coated.
- Spread the almonds in single layer on a baking sheet.
- Bake at 250 degrees for 1 hour, tossing every 15 minutes.

Makes 4 cups

Candied Walnuts

3   tablespoons sugar
2   teaspoons salt
1½   teaspoons freshly ground black pepper
1   teaspoon cumin
1   teaspoon cinnamon
       Pinch of cayenne pepper
6   tablespoons light corn syrup
1   pound walnuts

- Combine the sugar, salt, black pepper, cumin, cinnamon and cayenne pepper in a bowl and mix well.
- Add the corn syrup and mix well.
- Add the walnuts and toss until coated. Spread in single layer on a baking sheet sprayed with nonstick cooking spray.
- Bake at 325 degrees for 15 minutes or until the walnuts are deep golden brown and coating is bubbly, stirring every 5 minutes.
- Let stand on the baking sheet until cool.

Makes 5 cups

Note: Candied Walnuts make lovely Christmas or hostess gifts for family and friends when wrapped. They are great served on a salad or with fruit. May substitute pecan halves for the walnuts.

Spiced-Up Nuts

2   teaspoons Chinese five-spice powder
2   teaspoons cinnamon
2   teaspoons ginger
2   teaspoons cumin
2   teaspoons salt
1   teaspoon chile powder (preferably chipotle chile powder)
1/2   teaspoon garlic powder
2   egg whites
8   cups mixed nuts (pecans, walnuts, cashews, macadamias)
1/4   cup sugar
1 1/2 cups julienned strips crystallized ginger, or more to taste
      Salt to taste (optional)

- Combine the five-spice powder, cinnamon, ginger, cumin, salt, chile powder and garlic powder in a small bowl and mix well.
- Whisk the egg whites in a large bowl until foamy.
- Add the spice mixture and whisk well.
- Add the nuts and toss until completely coated.
- Add the sugar and toss well.
- Divide the nut mixture among two baking parchment-lined baking sheets and spread out in a single layer.
- Bake at 225 degrees for 1 hour and 20 minutes or until dry and toasted, stirring every 20 minutes. Season with salt and toss.
- Place the nuts in a large bowl and stir in the crystallized ginger. Let stand until completely cool.

Makes 9 cups

Note: The crystallized ginger adds a pungent kick that makes these nuts disappear at any party. Store in airtight container at room temperature for up to one week. May be frozen.

Marinated Mozzarella

    4   garlic cloves, minced
    1   teaspoon minced fresh oregano
    1   teaspoon minced fresh marjoram
    1   teaspoon minced basil
    2   tablespoons drained capers
    1/2 teaspoon salt
    1/2 teaspoon crushed red pepper
    1/2 teaspoon freshly ground black pepper
    1   (8-ounce) jar oil-pack sun-dried tomatoes
    2   (4-ounce) fresh mozzarella cheese balls, sliced, or
         fresh pearl mozzarella cheese
    1   cup (about) extra-virgin olive oil
         Focaccia or crusty bread

- Combine the garlic, oregano, marjoram, basil and capers in a small bowl and mix well.

- Add the salt, crushed red pepper and black pepper and mix well.

- Drain and mince the sun-dried tomatoes, reserving the oil.

- Layer half the sun-dried tomatoes, half the spice mixture, cheese, remaining sun-dried tomatoes and spice mixture in a bowl.

- Drizzle with the reserved sun-dried tomato oil and olive oil, coating completely. Tap the bowl gently on the counter to release any air bubbles.

- Marinate, covered, in the refrigerator for 24 hours or longer. Serve with focaccia or crusty bread.

Serves 6

Note: The marinated cheese may be refrigerated in a sterilized jar for approximately one week.

It's Not Just Pimento Cheese

16 ounces sharp Cheddar
cheese, shredded

8 ounces Monterey Jack
cheese, shredded

6 slices bacon, crisp-cooked
and crumbled

1 tablespoon chopped
fresh parsley

1 tablespoon chopped
fresh chives

1/2 teaspoon dill weed

1/2 teaspoon celery seeds

3/4 cup mayonnaise

5 roasted red bell peppers,
minced (*see Note page 19*), or
1 (7-ounce) jar chopped
pimentos, drained
Freshly ground black pepper
to taste
Cayenne pepper to taste

■ Combine the Cheddar cheese and Monterey Jack cheese in a mixing bowl.
Add the bacon, parsley, chives, dill weed and celery seeds and mix well.

■ Add the mayonnaise and mix until combined. Fold in the red peppers. Season with
black pepper and cayenne pepper. If serving as a dip, add additional mayonnaise
as needed to reach the desired consistency. Store in the refrigerator.

Serves 20

Cheese Pear

14 ounces sharp Cheddar
cheese, shredded

8 ounces Monterey Jack
cheese, shredded

8 ounces cream cheese, softened

4 ounces Roquefort cheese,
softened

1 cup pecans, toasted
and chopped

2 garlic cloves, minced
Hot red pepper sauce to taste
Paprika
Cinnamon stick,
cut into 3 pieces

■ Combine the Cheddar cheese, Monterey Jack cheese, cream cheese, Roquefort
cheese, pecans, garlic and hot sauce in a bowl and mix well. Divide the mixture
into three equal portions and shape each into a pear. Smooth the surface and
dust with paprika. Place a piece of cinnamon stick on the top for a stem.

■ Chill, covered, until serving time. Let stand at room temperature for 20 minutes
before serving. Serve on oiled green leaves or paper leaves, if desired.

Serves 18

Mock Goat Cheese

8 ounces cream cheese, softened
4 ounces crumbled feta cheese
2 teaspoons chopped fresh parsley
1 tablespoon freshly ground pepper

- Combine the cream cheese, feta cheese, parsley and pepper in a bowl and mix well.
- Freeze for 15 minutes before serving.

Makes 1 1/2 cups

Herb Cheese Spread

1 cup (2 sticks) butter, softened
16 ounces cream cheese, softened
2 garlic cloves, minced
1 teaspoon cracked pepper, or more to taste
1/2 teaspoon oregano
1/2 teaspoon basil
1/2 teaspoon thyme
1/2 teaspoon marjoram

- Whip the butter in a mixing bowl until light and fluffy.
- Add the cream cheese and mix well.
- Stir in the garlic, pepper, oregano, basil, thyme and marjoram.
- Chill, covered, until serving time.

Makes 3 cups

Note: This cheese spread is similar to Boursin Cheese Spread. It is delicious stuffed in mushroom caps, spread on toasted baguette slices, broiled on top of tomatoes, etc.

Apple Curry Spread

24 ounces cream cheese, softened
1 cup half-and-half
1/4 cup lemon juice
8 to 12 ounces mango chutney
1 tablespoon curry powder
1/2 cup chopped scallions
1 cup walnuts
1 cup dark raisins
6 Granny Smith apples, sliced, or ginger thins

- Process the cream cheese, half-and-half and lemon juice in a food processor until smooth.
- Add the chutney and curry powder and process until combined.
- Add the scallions, walnuts and raisins and pulse until well combined; do not overprocess. Store in the refrigerator.
- Serve with the Granny Smith apples or ginger thins.

Serves 15

Note: Soak the apple slices in orange juice or apple juice immediately after slicing to prevent browning. Drain and discard the juice before serving.

"What's This" Spread

2 cups mayonnaise
1 (8- to 10-ounce) jar stuffed olives, drained and finely chopped
1 cup pecans, toasted and finely chopped
1 small red onion, finely chopped
1 egg, hard-cooked and grated

- Mix the mayonnaise, olives, pecans, onion and egg in a bowl.
- Chill, covered, until serving time. Serve with crackers.

Makes 2 1/2 cups

Note: Store in the refrigerator for up to one week. This spread also makes pretty tea sandwiches. To prepare them in advance, cut bread into the desired shapes and freeze in plastic freezer-safe containers. Spread on thawed bread when ready to serve.

Garden Party Onion Sandwiches

2   loaves very thinly sliced white bread, crusts removed
8   ounces cream cheese, softened
     Homemade Mayonnaise (*below*)
2   large sweet onions, sliced paper thin
1/2 cup (1 stick) butter, melted

- Spread one side of half the bread with the cream cheese.
- Spread one side of the remaining bread with the Homemade Mayonnaise.
- Arrange the onion slices on mayonnaise-spread slices; top with cream cheese-spread slices.
- Brush both sides of the sandwiches with the butter.
- Cook on a griddle until toasted brown, turning once.
- Cut the sandwiches into halves. Serve immediately.

Serves 20

Homemade Mayonnaise

1/4 cup vegetable oil
1   egg
1 1/2 teaspoons Dijon mustard
1/4 teaspoon salt
     Juice of 1 lemon
3/4 cup (about) vegetable oil

- Process 1/4 cup oil, the egg, Dijon mustard, salt and lemon juice in a food processor with a steel blade until combined.
- Add 3/4 cup oil gradually, 1/4 cup at a time, processing constantly until thickened and of desired consistency. Store in the refrigerator.

Makes 1 1/2 cups

Note: If you are concerned about using raw eggs, use eggs pasteurized in their shells, which are sold at some specialty food stores, or use an equivalent amount of pasteurized egg substitute.

Sweet Almond Cheese Delight

1   envelope unflavored gelatin
1/4   cup cold water
12   ounces cream cheese, softened
4   ounces butter, softened
1/2   cup sour cream
1/2   cup sugar
1   cup slivered almonds, toasted
1/2   cup golden raisins
     Grated zest of 2 lemons
     Ginger thins or crackers

- Soften the gelatin in the water in a heat-proof bowl.
- Heat the gelatin mixture over hot water until the gelatin is dissolved, stirring constantly.
- Beat the cream cheese, butter, sour cream and sugar in a mixing bowl until light and fluffy.
- Add the gelatin mixture and mix well.
- Stir in the almonds, raisins and lemon zest. Spoon into a 1-quart mold.
- Chill, covered, until firm.
- Unmold onto a serving platter and serve with ginger thins or crackers.

Serves 12

Vegetable Mold

    2   cucumbers
    2   carrots
    1   onion, cut into quarters
    1   green bell pepper, cut into quarters
    1/2 cup coarsely chopped celery
    1   envelope unflavored gelatin
    1/4 cup water
    2   cups mayonnaise
    8   ounces cream cheese, softened
    2   tablespoons lemon juice
    2   teaspoons dried dill weed
         Small alfalfa sprouts
         Scored cucumber slices, crackers or Crostini (*page 69*)

- Peel, remove the seeds and cut the cucumbers into quarters.

- Peel and cut the carrots into halves.

- Process the cucumbers, carrots, onion, bell pepper and celery in a food processor until finely chopped.

- Sprinkle the gelatin over the water in a heat-proof bowl and let stand until softened.

- Heat the gelatin mixture over hot water until dissolved, stirring constantly.

- Combine the mayonnaise, cream cheese, lemon juice and dill weed in a bowl and mix well. Stir in the gelatin mixture.

- Stir in the chopped vegetable mixture and spoon into a mold.

- Chill, covered, until firm.

- Unmold onto a serving platter. Garnish with alfalfa sprouts. Serve with or on scored cucumber slices, crackers or Crostini.

Serves 12

Note: To score cucumbers, drag a fork down the length of the cucumber. You may also pour the mixture into a 10×15-inch rimmed pan. Chill, covered, until firm. Cut into shapes and place on lightly toasted bread cut into the same shapes. Tomato aspic can also be served this way.

Caviar Cake

1	envelope unflavored gelatin	2	tablespoons mayonnaise
1/4	cup cold water	1/2	teaspoon salt
4	hard-cooked eggs, chopped		Black pepper to taste
1/4	cup minced parsley		Dash of hot red pepper sauce
1	large green onion, chopped	1	cup sour cream
3/4	teaspoon salt	1/4	cup minced onion
3/4	teaspoon white pepper	1	(4-ounce) jar red or
	Dash of hot red pepper sauce		black caviar
2	avocados		Lemon juice
1	shallot, minced		Dark pumpernickel bread
2	tablespoons lemon juice		

- Line a 1-quart soufflé dish smoothly with aluminum foil or plastic wrap, extending 4 inches beyond the rim of the dish.

- Sprinkle the gelatin over the water in a heatproof measuring cup and let stand until softened. Place the measuring cup in a pan of hot water and stir until the gelatin is dissolved.

- Combine 1 tablespoon of the gelatin mixture, the eggs, parsley, green onion, 3/4 teaspoon salt, white pepper and hot sauce in a bowl and mix well. Adjust the seasonings as needed.

- Purée 1 avocado and chop the remaining avocado. Combine in a bowl.

- Add the shallot, 2 tablespoons lemon juice, the mayonnaise, 1/2 teaspoon salt, black pepper, hot sauce and 1 tablespoon of the gelatin mixture to the avocados. Mix well and adjust the seasonings as needed.

- Combine the sour cream, onion and remaining gelatin mixture in a bowl and mix well.

- Layer the egg mixture, the avocado mixture and the sour cream mixture in the prepared dish, spreading each layer evenly with a spatula before adding the next.

- Chill, covered tightly with plastic wrap, for 8 to 10 hours or longer.

- Rinse the caviar in a fine mesh strainer and sprinkle with lemon juice; drain.

- Unmold the congealed layers onto a serving plate and spread the caviar carefully on top. Serve with thinly sliced pumpernickel bread.

Serves 12

Apple Walnut Pâté

1	onion, chopped	1/4	cup brandy
3	large shallots, minced	8	ounces cream cheese, softened
2	garlic cloves, minced	1	cup walnuts, finely chopped
3	tablespoons butter	1/2	teaspoon salt
2	apples, peeled, cored and chopped	1/2	teaspoon tarragon
1	tablespoon butter	1/8	teaspoon thyme
1	pound chicken livers	1/8	teaspoon ground allspice
8	ounces hot sausages, casings removed		Crackers or apple slices

- Sauté the onion, shallots, and garlic in 3 tablespoons butter in a large skillet until translucent.

- Add the apples and sauté until tender. Remove the apple mixture from the skillet with a slotted spoon, reserving the pan drippings in the skillet.

- Melt 1 tablespoon butter in the skillet and add the chicken livers and sausages. Sauté until the chicken livers are cooked through and the sausage is brown and crumbly.

- Add the brandy and ignite. Flambé until the flame goes out.

- Remove from the heat and let stand until cool.

- Process the apple mixture and the chicken liver mixture in a food processor until puréed. Spoon the mixture into a bowl.

- Add the cream cheese, walnuts, salt, tarragon, thyme and allspice; mix well.

- Spoon into a mold smoothly lined with plastic wrap. Chill, covered, until set.

- Unmold onto a serving plate. Serve with crackers or apple slices.

Serves 20

Note: This is an elegant, yet inexpensive, appetizer that is worth the effort.

ACC Reuben Dip

32   ounces sauerkraut, drained
1   pound pastrami, chopped
16   ounces Swiss cheese, chopped
16   ounces cream cheese, softened
   Rye crackers or toasted rye bread
   Mustard (optional)

■ Combine the sauerkraut, pastrami, Swiss cheese and cream cheese in a bowl and mix well. Spoon into a baking dish.

■ Bake at 350 degrees for 45 minutes or until heated through.

■ Serve hot with rye crackers or toasted rye bread. Serve mustard on the side.

Serves 16

Smoked Trout Dip

1   pound smoked trout
8   ounces cream cheese
1/2   cup sour cream or mayonnaise
3   sprigs fresh dill weed, chopped
1   tablespoon rinsed and drained capers
   Salt and freshly ground pepper to taste
   Paprika
   Minced parsley
   Whole dill pickles, sliced into 1/2-inch rounds
   Crackers

■ Process the trout, cream cheese, sour cream, dill weed, capers, salt and pepper in a food processor until smooth.

■ Spoon into a serving bowl and sprinkle with paprika and parsley. Serve with the dill pickles and crackers.

Serves 10

Note: Many fishermen smoke their catch. This is a delectable way to showcase it. You may substitute smoked blue fish or smoked salmon for the trout.

Parsley's Green Sauce

2 cups mayonnaise
1/3 cup finely chopped parsley
1/3 cup finely chopped green onion tops (green part)
2 tablespoons finely chopped green onion bulbs (white part)
1/3 cup packed spinach leaves, minced
1/4 cup sour cream
1/4 cup fresh lemon juice
1/4 teaspoon Worcestershire sauce
Salt and freshly ground pepper to taste
Cooked shrimp or sliced vegetables

■ Combine the mayonnaise, parsley, green onions, spinach, sour cream, lemon juice and Worcestershire sauce in a bowl; mix well. Season with salt and pepper.

■ Chill, covered, until serving time. Serve with shrimp or vegetables.

Makes 3 cups

Shrimp with Southern Cocktail Sauce

1 cup mayonnaise
1/4 cup vegetable oil
2 tablespoons dry mustard
1 tablespoon horseradish
1 tablespoon chopped green onion
1 tablespoon chopped celery
1 tablespoon chopped parsley
1 tablespoon vinegar
1 teaspoon paprika
1/2 teaspoon salt
1/2 teaspoon Worcestershire sauce
Dash of hot red pepper sauce
2 pounds cooked shrimp, peeled and deveined

■ Pulse the mayonnaise, oil, dry mustard, horseradish, green onion, celery, parsley, vinegar, paprika, salt, Worcestershire sauce and hot sauce in a food processor until smooth. Spoon into a bowl.

■ Chill, covered, until ready to serve. Place the bowl on a serving platter and arrange the shrimp around the sauce.

Serves 6

Note: This sauce may be doubled and stored in a container with a tight-fitting lid in the refrigerator for two to three months. May also be used on meat sandwiches or as a dressing for a seafood salad.

Roasted Garlic Dip

12	large unpeeled garlic cloves
3	tablespoons peanut oil
8	ounces cream cheese, softened
1/4	cup sour cream
2	teaspoons Worcestershire sauce
1/2	teaspoon Dijon mustard
3	tablespoons coarsely chopped blanched almonds
2	tablespoons minced shallots
2	tablespoons chopped fresh parsley
1	teaspoon dried rosemary
1/2	teaspoon cardamom
1/4	teaspoon freshly ground pepper
1/3	cup heavy whipping cream
	Crostini (*page 69*)

- Toss the garlic with the peanut oil on a baking sheet, coating well.

- Bake at 300 degrees for 40 minutes or until deep golden brown.

- Let stand for 20 minutes or until cool; peel the cloves.

- Pulse the garlic with any excess peanut oil on the baking sheet in a food processor until chopped.

- Add the cream cheese, sour cream, Worcestershire sauce and Dijon mustard and process until smooth. Spoon into a bowl.

- Stir in the almonds, shallots, parsley, rosemary, cardamom and pepper.

- Beat the cream until firm peaks form. Fold into the garlic mixture.

- Chill, covered, for 1 hour. Serve with Crostini.

Makes 2 cups

Ginger Dip

1   cup mayonnaise
1   cup sour cream
1   (4-ounce) can water
     chestnuts, drained
     and chopped
1/4   cup minced green onions

1/4   cup minced fresh parsley
2   tablespoons chopped
     candied ginger
1   tablespoon soy sauce
     Rice crackers

- Combine the mayonnaise, sour cream, water chestnuts, green onions, parsley, candied ginger and soy sauce in a bowl and mix well.
- Chill, covered, until serving time. Serve with rice crackers.

Makes 2 1/2 cups

Note: The candied ginger adds a pungent kick to this dip.

Vegetables with Wasabi Mayonnaise

2   pounds asparagus
1   cup mayonnaise
4   teaspoons soy sauce
1   tablespoon wasabi paste,
     or to taste

2   teaspoons fresh lemon juice,
     or to taste
1 1/2 teaspoons sugar
2   red bell peppers, sliced
     into strips

- Snap off the woody ends of the asparagus spears.
- Blanch the asparagus in boiling water for 1 minute or until bright green. Drain and immediately rinse under cold running water until cool; drain and pat dry. Chill the asparagus until serving time.
- Combine the mayonnaise, soy sauce, wasabi paste, lemon juice and sugar in a bowl and whisk until the sugar is dissolved. Chill, covered, until serving time.
- Spoon the wasabi mayonnaise into a serving bowl and place on a serving platter. Arrange the asparagus and bell peppers on the platter around the mayonnaise.

Serves 6

Note: This sauce may be made one day ahead. Serve the sauce with shrimp or any assortment of blanched vegetables.

Seven-Layer Dip

1   pound mild chorizo sausage links, casings removed
8   ounces sour cream
3   tablespoons basil pesto
2   tablespoons sun-dried tomato pesto (optional)
1   teaspoon garlic powder
1   (15-ounce) can black beans, drained and rinsed
1   (7-ounce) can mild green chiles, drained
1   (14-ounce) can diced tomatoes, drained
1/2 cup (2 ounces) grated sharp Cheddar cheese
1   (4-ounce) jar chopped pimentos, drained
4   green onions, chopped
1/2 cup (2 ounces) freshly grated Parmesan cheese
    Tortilla chips

■ Sauté the sausage in a skillet until cooked through. Drain and cut into bite-size pieces.

■ Combine the sour cream, basil pesto, sun-dried tomato pesto and garlic powder in a bowl and mix well.

■ Layer the sausage, black beans, green chiles, tomatoes, Cheddar cheese, pimentos, green onions, sour cream mixture and Parmesan cheese in a baking dish.

■ Bake at 350 degrees for 30 minutes or until bubbly. Serve warm with tortilla chips.

Serves 8

Note: The pesto makes this seven-layer dip special.

Jazz Under the Stars

Daylight saving time is the harbinger of boating season. The Intracoastal
Waterway becomes a mecca for south-to-north travelers who stop frequently in
Wrightsvillle Beach on their way to cooler climates. Why not start your
season with a Jazz Under the Stars party, a cocktail party featuring good food,
live jazz, and special friends.

Cheese Pear
Spicy Hot Almonds

Poached Salmon with Lemon Cucumber Sauce
Beef Tenderloin with Horseradish Sauce
BLT New Potatoes
Ham and Okra Roll-Ups
Confetti Shrimp
Vegetables with Wasabi Mayonnaise

Pecan Clusters
Almond Macaroons

Elisabeth Chant (English, 1865–1947)
Compositions: Pre-Gothic Days in Devon, n.d.
Watercolor on paper
Gift of Henry MacMillian

Soups & Breads

The Cook's Canvas 2

Summer Melon Soup

2   ripe cantaloupes
$1/3$ cup fresh orange juice
$1/3$ cup apple juice
$1/4$ cup sugar
$1/4$ cup dry sherry
1   tablespoon lime juice
1   tablespoon fresh lemon juice
1   tablespoon grated fresh ginger, or to taste
1   teaspoon vanilla extract
     Lime slices

- Purée peeled and chopped cantaloupes $1/2$ at a time in food processor fitted with a steel blade.

- Combine the cantaloupe purée, orange juice, apple juice, sugar, sherry, lime juice, lemon juice, ginger and vanilla in a bowl; mix well.

- Chill, covered, for 2 to 10 hours.

- Ladle into chilled soup bowls and garnish with lime slices.

Serves 6 to 8

Note: Fresh blueberries make a colorful addition and provide added texture.

Hearts of Palm Soup

2   tablespoons butter
1/2 onion, chopped
1/2 cup chopped celery with leaves
1   garlic clove, chopped
2¹/2 cups chicken stock
1/2 cup white wine
1   (14-ounce) can hearts of palm, drained and chopped
1   cup heavy cream
1   avocado
     Juice of 1 lemon
     Lemon slices

- Melt the butter over low heat in a saucepan and add the onion, celery and garlic. Cook until the onion is translucent.
- Stir in the stock, wine and hearts of palm. Bring to a boil and reduce the heat. Cook, covered, over low heat for 35 minutes, stirring occasionally.
- Purée the soup in a food processor fitted with a steel blade. Pour the purée into a bowl and stir in the cream. Chill, covered, for 2 to 10 hours.
- Cut the avocado into halves and discard the pit. Scoop small balls from the pulp using a melon baller. Gently toss the avocado with the lemon juice in a bowl.
- Ladle the soup into chilled soup bowls and garnish each with a lemon slice and the avocado balls.

Serves 4

Note: To give the soup the best flavor, use homemade stock or the best stock available. Serve with Walnut Roquefort Shortbread (page 70).

Cold Tomato Soup

3	cups tomato juice
1/2	cup finely minced green onions
2	tablespoons sun-dried tomato paste
2	tablespoons lemon juice
1	tablespoon minced fresh thyme
1/2	teaspoon (or more) curry powder
1/2	teaspoon finely grated lemon zest
1/2	teaspoon freshly ground pepper
1/4	teaspoon salt
1	cup sour cream
1	teaspoon sugar
4	sprigs of thyme

- Combine the tomato juice, green onions, sun-dried tomato paste, lemon juice, thyme, curry powder, lemon zest, pepper and salt in a bowl and mix well. Chill, covered, for 2 to 10 hours.
- Mix the sour cream and sugar in a small bowl.
- Stir the sour cream mixture into the soup just before serving. Adjust the seasonings to taste.
- Ladle into chilled soup bowls and top each serving with a sprig of thyme.

Serves 4

Note: *For a richer soup, top with lump crab meat.*

Sweet Potato Vichyssoise

1   pound sweet potatoes
2   cups (1/4-inch) sliced leeks (*see Note*)
1/4 teaspoon grated fresh ginger
1/4 teaspoon grated fresh nutmeg
3   tablespoons butter
1 1/2 to 3 cups chicken stock
1 1/2 cups coconut milk
1   cup heavy cream
     Salt and freshly ground pepper to taste
     Crème fraîche or sour cream
1/4 cup chopped macadamia nuts, toasted

- Peel the sweet potatoes and cut into uniform pieces.
- Sauté the leeks with the ginger and nutmeg in the butter in a saucepan until the leeks are wilted but not brown. Stir in the sweet potatoes and add just enough stock to cover.
- Simmer until the sweet potatoes are tender, stirring occasionally.
- Combine the sweet potato mixture, coconut milk and cream in a blender and process until puréed. Season with salt and pepper.
- Pour the soup into a bowl and chill, covered, for 8 to 10 hours.
- Ladle into chilled soup bowls and top with crème fraîche and macadamia nuts.

Serves 8

Note: Trim roots and tough green leaves from leeks. Split leeks lengthwise approximately 1 inch from root ends and spread layers under cold running water, washing out any grit. Pat dry with paper towels. Cut the bulb into slices.

Creamy Artichoke Soup

3	tablespoons unsalted butter
1/2	cup sliced onion
3	shallots, sliced
2	garlic cloves, chopped
12	cups chicken stock
8	ounces small yellow potatoes, peeled and sliced
4	sprigs of parsley
4	sprigs of cilantro
1/4	teaspoon cracked pepper
7	canned artichoke bottoms
3	tablespoons unsalted butter
1/2	cup cream
	Salt to taste
	Chopped parsley

- Melt 3 tablespoons butter in a stockpot and add the onion, shallots and garlic. Cook until the onions are tender but not brown. Stir in the stock, potatoes, parsley, cilantro and pepper.
- Simmer for 30 minutes, stirring occasionally. Add the artichokes and simmer for 30 minutes longer.
- Purée the artichoke mixture in batches in a food processor.
- Reheat the artichoke purée in a stockpot and whisk in 3 tablespoons butter and the cream. Season with salt.
- Ladle into soup bowls and garnish with chopped parsley.

Serves 8

Note: *To give soups the best flavor, use homemade stock or the best quality stock available.*

Butternut Squash Bisque

1   cup chopped onion
1   cup chopped celery
1   cup chopped carrots
$1/2$ cup (1 stick) butter
5   cups coarsely chopped butternut squash
2   sweet potatoes, peeled and chopped
5   cups chicken stock
$1^1/2$ cups packed light brown sugar
$3/4$ cup maple syrup
2   cups heavy cream
    Salt and freshly ground pepper to taste
    Freshly ground nutmeg to taste
    Edible flowers

- Sauté the onion, celery and carrots in the butter in a saucepan until tender. Stir in the squash and sweet potatoes.

- Sauté for 10 to 15 minutes over medium heat. Stir in the stock, brown sugar and syrup. Simmer until the sweet potatoes and squash are tender-crisp.

- Process the squash mixture in batches in a food processor until the vegetables are finely chopped.

- Return the squash mixture to the saucepan and stir in the cream. Simmer until heated through and season with salt and pepper.

- Ladle into soup bowls and sprinkle with nutmeg. Garnish each serving with an edible flower.

Serves 8

Note: *Serve with Cumin Pepper Crisps (page 68).*

Orange Carrot Soup

2 tablespoons olive oil
1 yellow onion, coarsely chopped
1 rib celery, coarsely chopped
1 leek bulb, chopped (*see Note page 49*)
15 carrots, peeled and cut into large chunks
4 cups vegetable broth or water
1/4 cup fresh orange juice
2 tablespoons minced fresh ginger
1 cup half-and-half or heavy cream
Salt and freshly ground pepper to taste

■ Heat the olive oil in a Dutch oven and add the onion, celery and leek. Cook, covered, over medium heat until the vegetables are tender. Add the carrots and continue to cook until the carrots are tender-crisp.

■ Add the broth, orange juice and ginger. Simmer until the carrots are very tender.

■ Purée the carrot mixture in batches in a blender or food processor; return the purée to the saucepan.

■ Stir in the half-and-half. Simmer just until heated through. Season with salt and pepper and ladle into soup bowls.

Serves 8

Note: Curry Butter Toast Sticks are a great complement to most any soup. Blend 1/4 cup butter with 1/2 teaspoon curry powder. Trim the crusts from bread slices and cut each slice into three strips. Toast until light brown. Spread the curry mixture on one side of each toasted strip and broil until the edges are crisp.

Santa Fe Corn Chowder

1	tablespoon olive oil
1	onion, chopped
1	red or green bell pepper, chopped
3	large ribs celery, chopped
4	garlic cloves, minced
3	cups fresh or frozen whole kernel corn
1	(4-ounce) can chopped mild green chiles
1	(4-ounce) jar chopped pimentos
2	tablespoons chopped fresh parsley
1	tablespoon ground coriander
1	teaspoon ground cumin
1/4	teaspoon hot red pepper flakes
	Salt to taste
1/4	cup (1/2 stick) butter
1/4	cup all-purpose flour
6	cups milk, heated
8	slices bacon, crisp-cooked and crumbled

- Heat the olive oil in a stockpot. Add the onion, bell pepper, celery and garlic and sauté until the onion is tender.
- Add the corn, green chiles, pimentos, parsley, coriander, cumin, red pepper flakes and salt. Simmer for 30 minutes, stirring occasionally.
- Melt the butter in a saucepan and stir in the flour with a wooden spoon to make a roux. Cook for 5 minutes or until golden brown, stirring constantly. Whisk in the milk and cook until thickened, stirring frequently.
- Add to the corn mixture and simmer just until heated through.
- Ladle into soup bowls and top with the bacon.

Serves 8 to 10

Note: The flavor of the soup is enhanced if prepared one day in advance and stored, covered, in the refrigerator. Reheat before serving.

Wild Mushroom Soup

1	pound shiitake mushrooms, or a mixture of portobello, button and shiitake mushrooms
6	cups chicken stock
1	tablespoon olive oil
3	ribs celery, chopped
1	onion, chopped
2	carrots, chopped
2	leek bulbs, chopped (*see Note page 49*)

2	garlic cloves, crushed
	Salt and freshly ground pepper to taste
6	tablespoons unsalted butter
1/2	cup all-purpose flour
1	tablespoon unsalted butter
1	(14-ounce) can diced tomatoes, drained
1	cup heavy cream

- Remove the stems from the mushrooms, reserving the stems. Slice enough caps to measure 3 cups and reserve.

- Combine the reserved mushroom stems and the remaining mushroom caps with the stock in a stockpot and bring to a boil. Reduce the heat and simmer for 30 minutes.

- Heat the olive oil in a saucepan and add the celery, onion, carrots, leeks and garlic. Sauté over medium heat for 5 minutes or until the onion is translucent. Season with salt and pepper. Stir the vegetable mixture into the stock mixture and simmer for several minutes.

- Melt 6 tablespoons butter in a small saucepan over low heat. Stir in the flour gradually to make a roux. Cook for 5 minutes or until bubbly and smooth, stirring constantly. Strain 4 cups of the stock mixture into the roux and whisk until blended. Add to the stockpot and mix well.

- Simmer over low heat for 20 minutes. Remove from heat. Purée the mushroom mixture in a food processor fitted with a steel blade. Return the purée to the stockpot and heat over medium-low heat.

- Melt 1 tablespoon butter in a saucepan over medium heat and stir in the 3 cups reserved mushroom caps. Sauté for 5 minutes. Stir in the tomatoes and cook for 5 minutes. Season with salt and pepper. Add the cream and cook just until heated through; do not boil.

- Add the cream mixture to the stockpot and mix well. Ladle into soup bowls.

Serves 8

Creamy Tomato Herb Soup

2   tablespoons butter
2 1/2 cups chopped onions
2   garlic cloves, minced
1   teaspoon salt
1   teaspoon chopped fresh rosemary
1   teaspoon chopped fresh basil
1   (28-ounce) can crushed tomatoes
1   (14-ounce) can chicken broth
6   tablespoons sherry
1/2   teaspoon honey
8   ounces cream cheese, cubed
      Sprigs of parsley

- Melt the butter in a large saucepan. Add the onions and garlic and sauté until the onions are translucent.
- Stir in the salt, rosemary and basil. Sauté for 2 minutes.
- Add the tomatoes, broth, sherry and honey and mix well. Simmer, covered, for 30 to 40 minutes, stirring occasionally.
- Add the cream cheese. Cook until melted and blended, stirring frequently.
- Ladle into soup bowls and garnish with parsley.

Serves 4

Note: For a cold winter night meal, serve with Cheddar Scallion Drop Biscuits (page 75) and a tossed green salad.

Roasted Vegetable Soup with Basil

1   eggplant
        Olive oil for coating
1   zucchini, cut into large chunks
1   large yellow squash, cut into large chunks
1   red onion, cut into quarters
6   Roma tomatoes, cut lengthwise into halves
2   tablespoons olive oil
2   garlic cloves, minced
1   red bell pepper, roasted, chopped (*see Note page 19*)
4   to 6 cups vegetable stock
1/2   cup (or more) fresh basil
        Salt and freshly ground pepper to taste
        Microwave Croutons (*page 70*)
        Freshly grated Parmesan cheese

- Cut the eggplant lengthwise into halves. Prick the peel with a fork and coat with olive oil. Arrange the eggplant halves on a baking sheet.

- Roast at 400 degrees for 30 minutes or until tender and light brown. Let stand until cool. Remove the peel and cut into large chunks. Maintain the oven temperature.

- Combine the zucchini, yellow squash and onion with enough olive oil to coat in a bowl. Arrange the zucchini mixture in a single layer on a baking sheet and roast for 30 minutes or until the vegetables are tender and light brown. Maintain the oven temperature.

- Toss the tomatoes with enough olive oil to coat in a bowl. Arrange the tomatoes on a baking sheet and roast for 15 minutes.

- Heat 2 tablespoons olive oil in a heavy stockpot and add the garlic. Cook for 1 minute. Add the eggplant, zucchini mixture, tomatoes, bell pepper and enough of the stock to cover. Bring to a boil and reduce the heat.

- Simmer for 30 to 40 minutes or until of the desired consistency, adding additional stock if needed for a thinner consistency. Stir in the basil, salt and pepper.

- Ladle into soup bowls and top with the Microwave Croutons. Serve with Parmesan cheese.

Serves 8

Minestrone

1   tablespoon olive oil
2   zucchini, chopped
1   onion, chopped
2   carrots, sliced
1   leek, chopped (*see Note page 49*)
2   ribs celery, chopped
1   garlic clove, minced
8   cups vegetable broth or chicken broth
1   (28-ounce) can diced tomatoes
1/2 cup orzo
1   (14-ounce) can cannellini beans, drained
1   (6-ounce) package frozen peas
    Salt and freshly ground pepper to taste
    Pesto
    Freshly grated Parmesan cheese (optional)

- Heat the olive oil in a stockpot over medium heat and stir in the zucchini, onion, carrots, leek, celery and garlic. Sauté until the vegetables are tender. Stir in the broth, tomatoes and pasta.

- Simmer, covered, for 45 minutes. Stir in the beans and peas and simmer for 10 minutes. Season with salt and pepper.

- Spoon a dollop of pesto in the bottom of each soup bowl and ladle the soup over the pesto. Sprinkle with Parmesan cheese.

Serves 8 to 10

Note: Using a vegetable peeler, shave long swirls of Parmesan cheese instead of grated Parmesan cheese to "dress up" the soup.

Vegetable Chili

2 cups sliced portobello and shiitake mushrooms
1 cup chopped onion
1 cup chopped yellow squash
1 cup chopped red and green bell pepper
2 to 4 teaspoons chili powder, or to taste
1/4 cup water
1 (19-ounce) can cannellini beans
1 (15-ounce) can red kidney beans
1 (15-ounce) can garbanzo beans
2 cups marinara sauce
1/4 cup bulgur or quinoa
   Frozen soy burger or sausage crumbles
   Vegetable stock or water
   Salt and freshly ground pepper to taste

- Combine the mushrooms, onion, squash, bell pepper, 2 teaspoons of the chili powder and the water in a stockpot and mix well. Simmer over medium heat for 5 minutes or until the vegetables are slightly tender.

- Add the undrained beans and marinara sauce and mix well. Simmer for 8 minutes, stirring occasionally.

- Add the bulgur and cook for 10 minutes or until the bulgur is tender, stirring frequently. Stir in the soy crumbles and cook just until heated through, adding additional stock for a thinner consistency.

- Taste and stir in the remaining 2 teaspoons chili powder, if desired. Season with salt and pepper and ladle into soup bowls.

Serves 12

Note: If the chili is too spicy, cut the heat with a little sugar. Vegetable stock is easy to prepare by just adding the concentrated powders available at natural food markets to water.

Meaty Minestrone

3/4 cup dried kidney beans
7 cups water
1 (16-ounce) can diced tomatoes
2 pounds beef stew meat, cut into 1-inch pieces
1/2 head cabbage, coarsely chopped
1 large carrot, sliced
1 large onion, sliced
2 garlic cloves, minced
2 teaspoons basil
1 teaspoon salt
1/4 teaspoon freshly ground pepper
1 (10-ounce) package frozen cut green beans
1/2 cup elbow macaroni
Freshly grated Parmesan cheese

- Sort and rinse the kidney beans.
- Combine the kidney beans and water in a stockpot and bring to a boil. Boil for 2 minutes and remove from the heat. Let stand, covered, for 1 hour.
- Drain the liquid from the tomatoes into the kidney beans, reserving the tomatoes. Stir in the stew meat, cabbage, carrot, onion, garlic, basil, salt and pepper.
- Simmer, covered, for 2 hours or until the stew meat is tender.
- Add the reserved tomatoes, green beans and pasta and mix well. Simmer for 15 to 20 minutes or until the pasta is tender. Ladle into soup bowls and top with Parmesan cheese.

Serves 6

Note: Flavor vegetable or meaty soups with the rind of fresh Parmesan cheese; discard the rind before serving. You may pour the soup into a large container, tie with a festive bow, and deliver as a housewarming gift.

Drunken Chili

2 pounds ground beef
3 tablespoons olive oil
3 onions, chopped
2 (14-ounce) cans whole
  tomatoes, drained
1 (12-ounce) can beer
1 (6-ounce) can mild green
  chiles, chopped
1 (6-ounce) can tomato paste
1/2 cup sugar
1/2 cup burgundy
5 garlic cloves, minced
2 tablespoons sun-dried
  tomato paste
1 tablespoon dried oregano
1 tablespoon dried
  ground cumin
1 tablespoon chili powder
1 tablespoon dried thyme
1 tablespoon dried basil
1 tablespoon paprika
1 tablespoon baking cocoa
1 teaspoon salt, or to taste
1/4 teaspoon ground cloves
2 bay leaves
2 dashes of hot red pepper sauce
2 (15-ounce) cans red kidney
  beans, drained
2 (15-ounce) cans black
  beans, drained
  Sour cream
  Cheddar cheese, shredded
  It's Not Just Pimento Cheese
  sandwiches (*page 30*)

■ Brown the ground beef in a stockpot, stirring until crumbly; drain. Add the olive oil and onions and cook for 5 minutes. Stir in the tomatoes, beer, green chiles, tomato paste, sugar and burgundy.

■ Add the garlic, sun-dried tomato paste, oregano, cumin, chili powder, thyme, basil, paprika, baking cocoa, salt, cloves, bay leaves and hot sauce; mix well.

■ Simmer for 45 minutes or until of the desired consistency, stirring occasionally. Add the beans and cook for 15 minutes longer, stirring occasionally. Discard the bay leaves.

■ Ladle into soup bowls and serve with sour cream and Cheddar cheese. Serve grilled It's Not Just Pimento Cheese sandwiches (*page 30*) on the side.

Serves 12

Note: *The flavor is enhanced if prepared one day in advance and stored, covered, in the refrigerator. Reheat before serving.*

Bacon and Celery Soup

2 slices bacon, chopped
2 tablespoons butter
6 cups chopped celery
1 1/2 cups chopped leeks (*see Note page 49*)
1 tablespoon minced fresh basil
4 cups chicken broth
2 tablespoons butter
2 tablespoons all-purpose flour
1 cup milk, heated
   Salt and freshly ground pepper to taste

- Cook the bacon in a skillet until brown and crisp. Drain, reserving 2 tablespoons of the drippings.

- Heat the reserved bacon drippings and 2 tablespoons butter in a saucepan until the butter melts. Add the celery, leeks and basil. Sauté for 5 to 8 minutes or until the vegetables are tender-crisp.

- Stir in the broth and simmer for 10 to 15 minutes or until the vegetables are tender, stirring occasionally.

- Melt 2 tablespoons butter in a saucepan and stir in the flour to make a roux. Cook until smooth and bubbly, stirring constantly. Add the milk gradually, stirring constantly. Cook for several minutes or until thickened. Stir the sauce into the celery mixture and cook just until heated through.

- Add the bacon and season with salt and pepper. Ladle into soup bowls.

- For a smooth soup, cool the celery mixture slightly and purée two-thirds of the mixture in a blender. Return the purée to the saucepan and stir in the bacon. Cook just until heated through. Season with salt and pepper and ladle into soup bowls.

Serves 6

Note: *Homemade soup is always better the next day as this allows the flavors to blend. Add additional broth or stock if the consistency is too thick.*

Roasted Shallot and Smoked Bacon Soup

1 pound unpeeled shallots, cut into quarters
1/4 cup olive oil
  Salt and freshly ground pepper to taste
1 pound hickory-smoked bacon, chopped
1 onion, chopped
2 ribs celery, chopped
6 cups chicken stock
6 tablespoons unsalted butter
3/4 cup all-purpose flour

- Arrange the shallots on a baking sheet. Drizzle with the olive oil and sprinkle with salt and pepper. Roast at 275 degrees for 20 minutes. Let stand until cool.

- Peel the shallots. Chop half the shallots into 1/4-inch pieces and reserve.

- Cook the bacon in a small stockpot until brown but not crisp. Remove the bacon with a slotted spoon to paper towels to drain. Reserve 2 tablespoons of the bacon drippings.

- Sauté the unchopped shallots, onion, celery, salt and pepper in the reserved bacon drippings for 5 minutes or until the onion is translucent. Stir in the stock and bring to a boil.

- Melt the butter in a saucepan over low heat. Stir in the flour to make a roux. Cook for 5 minutes or until bubbly and light brown and roux forms, stirring constantly. Strain 4 cups of the stock mixture into the roux, whisking until smooth. Whisk into the vegetable mixture until blended.

- Bring to a boil and reduce the heat. Simmer for 15 minutes and remove from the heat.

- Purée the vegetable mixture in a food processor fitted with a steel blade. Return the purée to the stockpot and simmer over medium heat.

- Sauté the bacon and chopped shallots in a skillet over medium heat for 3 minutes. Add to the soup. Ladle into soup bowls and serve immediately.

Serves 8

Cheddar Cheese and Bacon Soup

8   ounces bacon, cut into 1-inch pieces
10 tablespoons butter
2   red onions, finely chopped
1   cup finely chopped celery
1   leek, finely chopped (*see Note page 49*)
1¹/₂ cups all-purpose flour
4   cups chicken stock
5   cups milk, heated
1   pound Cheddar cheese, shredded
1   tablespoon Worcestershire sauce
1¹/₂ teaspoons hot red pepper sauce
    Kosher salt and freshly ground pepper to taste
1   teaspoon ale, slightly warm

- Brown the bacon in a stockpot. Add the butter and heat until the butter melts. Add the onions, celery and leek and sauté until tender.
- Stir in the flour to make a roux. Add the stock and simmer for 3 minutes.
- Stir in the milk. Cook until thickened, stirring constantly. Reduce the heat to low and add the cheese. Cook until the cheese melts. Stir in the Worcestershire sauce, hot sauce, salt and pepper.
- Stir in the ale just before serving. Ladle into soup bowls.

Serves 12

Note: When reheating the soup, do not bring to a boil as the high heat will cause the soup to separate. Serve with Cheddar Scallion Drop Biscuits (page 75).

Tasso and Lima Bean Soup

1   cup chopped celery
1   cup chopped onion
2   garlic cloves, minced
1/4 cup olive oil
1   pound tasso ham, finely chopped
10   cups chicken stock
6   cups frozen baby lima beans, thawed
     Salt and freshly ground pepper to taste

- Sauté the celery, onion and garlic in the olive oil in a stockpot over medium heat until tender. Reserve 1 cup of the ham. Stir the remaining ham into the celery mixture. Add the stock and bring to a boil.

- Add the beans and simmer until the beans are tender, stirring occasionally. Season with salt and pepper.

- Process the soup in batches in a blender until the vegetables and ham are finely chopped. Strain through a sieve into the stockpot, discarding the solids. Simmer just until heated through, stirring occasionally.

- Ladle into soup bowls and top with the reserved 1 cup ham.

Serves 6

Note: Press the cooked solids through a sieve using a wooden spoon. Work in small batches and discard the solids frequently.

Elwood's Ham Chowder

1   tablespoon vegetable oil
1   pound Virginia ham, cut into 1/2-inch pieces
2   large onions, cut into 1/2-inch pieces (about 3 cups)
4   garlic cloves, thinly sliced
1   pound frozen chopped collard greens, thawed
7   cups chicken stock or canned chicken broth
2   cups beef stock or canned beef broth
8   red potatoes, cut into 1/2-inch pieces (about 6 cups)
1   (28-ounce) can diced tomatoes
1 1/2 tablespoons chopped fresh thyme leaves
1 1/2 tablespoons chopped fresh flat-leaf parsley
     Salt and freshly ground pepper to taste
     Hot red pepper sauce (optional)

- Heat the oil in a large stockpot over medium-low heat. Add the ham and cook for 2 minutes or until the ham begins to release its juices; do not brown.

- Add the onions and garlic and cook for 10 minutes or until the onions are tender, stirring occasionally.

- Add the collard greens in batches and cook until wilted, tossing frequently with tongs. Stir in the stocks, potatoes, undrained tomatoes, thyme and parsley. Bring to a boil and reduce the heat to low.

- Simmer for 30 to 40 minutes or until the potatoes are tender, stirring occasionally. Skim any foam from the surface. Season with salt, pepper and hot sauce.

- Ladle into soup bowls.

Serves 8

Note: Serve with Johnny Cakes (page 73). Two bunches of coarsely chopped trimmed fresh collard greens may be substituted for the frozen collard greens.

Five-Star Chicken Soup

2   tablespoons butter
1   large sweet onion, chopped
2   large garlic cloves, minced
1   large red bell pepper, chopped
1   small jalapeño chile, seeded and chopped
2   large Granny Smith apples, peeled and chopped
2   teaspoons medium curry powder
2   tablespoons all-purpose flour
2   teaspoons minced fresh ginger
4   cups chicken stock
     Salt and freshly ground pepper to taste
2   cups chopped cooked chicken or turkey
1   cup half-and-half

- Melt the butter in a large saucepan and add the onion and garlic. Sauté for 5 minutes. Stir in the bell pepper and jalapeño chile.

- Sauté for 5 minutes. Add the apples and curry powder and mix well. Cook for 3 minutes, stirring frequently.

- Sprinkle the flour over the apple mixture and mix well. Cook for 3 minutes and stir in the ginger and stock. Season with salt and pepper. Bring to a boil over high heat and reduce the heat to low. Simmer for 15 minutes, stirring occasionally.

- Stir in the chicken or turkey and half-and-half and simmer for 10 minutes. Ladle into soup bowls.

- Best if prepared one to two days in advance and stored, covered, in the refrigerator. Reheat before serving.

Serves 8

Variation: *Substitute chicken and apple sausage for the chopped chicken, one 4-ounce can chopped green chiles for the jalapeño chile, and Fuji apples for the Granny Smith apples for a different taste.*

Hatteras Chowder

1   pound hot andouille sausage, cut into 1/4-inch pieces
1/4   cup (1/2 stick) butter
1   large onion, chopped
1   red bell pepper, chopped
1   yellow bell pepper, chopped
1/2   bunch celery, trimmed and chopped
6 1/2 cups water
2   large red-skinned potatoes, cut into cubes
1 1/2 cups seafood stock
1/2   cup sherry
2   tablespoons Cajun spice
2   tablespoons parsley flakes
1   tablespoon freshly ground pepper
1 1/2 pounds small shrimp, peeled and deveined
8   ounces backfin crab meat (*see Note page 22*)
1 1/2 cups water
1/2   cup cornstarch
1   tablespoon saffron

- Cook the sausage in the butter in a 2-gallon stockpot over medium-high heat until light brown. Stir in the onion, bell peppers and celery.
- Cook until the vegetables are tender-crisp. Stir in 6 1/2 cups water and the potatoes. Increase the heat to high and mix in the stock and sherry. Bring to a boil.
- Cook until the potatoes are tender. Stir in the Cajun spice, parsley flakes and pepper. Add the shrimp and crab meat and mix well.
- Whisk 1 1/2 cups water and the cornstarch in a bowl until blended and stir into the chowder. Dissolve the saffron in a small amount of water in a bowl and stir into the chowder. Simmer until the shrimp turn pink and the chowder thickens, stirring occasionally.
- Ladle into soup bowls.

Serves 16

Note: To prevent having a good cry when you are not in the mood, burn a candle near the cutting board when chopping onions.

Cumin Pepper Crisps

1   cup all-purpose flour
1/2   cup (1 stick) butter, softened
3   ounces Pepper Jack cheese, shredded
3   ounces Monterey Jack cheese, shredded
1   teaspoon ground cumin
1/4   teaspoon salt
2   teaspoons whole cumin seeds

- Combine the flour, butter, Pepper Jack cheese, Monterey Jack cheese, ground cumin and salt in a food processor. Pulse until the ingredients are combined and the mixture forms a ball.

- Shape the dough into a log 2 inches in diameter and 8 inches long. Wrap the log tightly in plastic wrap and roll on a hard surface to make compact. Freeze until firm. If not using immediately, the dough can be frozen for future use.

- Cut the log into 1/4-inch slices and arrange the slices 1 inch apart on an ungreased baking sheet. Press some of the whole cumin seeds in the top of each slice.

- Bake on the center oven rack at 400 degrees for 12 minutes or until light golden brown. Cool on the baking sheet for 5 minutes and remove to a wire rack.

- Serve warm or at room temperature. May be prepared up to one day in advance and stored in an airtight container at room temperature.

Makes 2 1/2 dozen

Note: It is nice to have "logs" in the freezer to pull out, slice, and bake for unexpected guests.

Toasted Pita Chips

12   whole pitas, split and separated into 24 rounds
      Extra-virgin olive oil to taste
      Dried oregano or parsley to taste
      Coarse salt and freshly ground pepper to taste

- Cut each pita round into fourths. Arrange the wedges rough side up in a single layer on a baking sheet.
- Combine olive oil, oregano, salt and pepper in the proportions desired and mix well.
- Brush the pita wedges with the olive oil mixture.
- Bake at 350 degrees for 12 to 15 minutes or until golden brown. Remove to a wire rack to cool.

Makes 8 dozen

Note: These chips can be stored in an airtight container for up to 1 week. Flour tortillas may be substituted for the pita rounds.

Crostini

1   small loaf Italian bread, thinly sliced
1/2 cup olive oil
1/2 cup (2 ounces) freshly grated Parmesan cheese

- Arrange the bread slices in a single layer on a baking sheet.
- Brush the slices with the olive oil and sprinkle with the cheese.
- Bake at 375 degrees for 10 minutes or until the cheese melts. Remove to a wire rack to cool.

Makes 3 dozen

Note: Serve as an appetizer, accompaniment to a salad, or on top of soups. Mix fresh herbs such as basil, sage, or thyme with the olive oil before brushing the bread slices, if desired.

Microwave Croutons

6   cups bread cubes (any type of bread can be used)
2   tablespoons Italian seasoning
1/2   teaspoon garlic salt
1/2   cup (1 stick) butter, melted

- Place the bread cubes in a 3-quart microwave-safe dish.
- Microwave for 6 minutes or until the cubes begin to dry out, stirring every 2 minutes.
- Sprinkle with the Italian seasoning and garlic salt and drizzle with the butter. Toss to coat. Microwave for 4 to 6 minutes or until the croutons are crisp, stirring every minute.

Makes 6 cups

Walnut Roquefort Shortbread

1 1/2 cups all-purpose flour
1   cup chopped walnuts
8   ounces Roquefort cheese, chilled and crumbled
1/2   cup (1 stick) butter
2   egg yolks
1   tablespoon freshly ground pepper

- Combine the flour, walnuts, cheese, butter, egg yolks and pepper in a food processor or electric mixer. Process until mixture forms a ball.
- Divide the dough into two equal portions and shape each portion into a log 1 1/2 inches in diameter.
- Wrap the logs in plastic wrap. Chill for 4 hours or for up to 3 days or store in the freezer for up to 1 month.
- Cut the logs into 1/2-inch rounds and arrange on an ungreased baking sheet.
- Bake at 425 degrees for 10 minutes or until light brown. Remove to paper towels to cool.
- Best eaten on the day baked.

Makes 2 dozen

Roquefort Popovers

1½ cups milk
8 ounces Roquefort cheese, crumbled
1 teaspoon salt
Freshly ground pepper to taste
2 cups all-purpose flour
6 eggs

- Generously grease a popover pan with vegetable oil or shortening.
- Set oven rack to the lowest position. Preheat oven to 400 degrees.
- Combine the milk and cheese in a saucepan and cook over medium-low heat until cheese melts, stirring frequently. Remove from the heat and whisk in the salt and pepper.
- Place the flour in a medium bowl and whisk in the cheese mixture just until combined; dough will be slightly lumpy.
- Add the eggs one at a time, whisking until blended after each addition.
- Pour the batter evenly into the prepared popover cups and bake for 20 minutes; do not open the oven door.
- Reduce the oven temperature to 350 degrees and bake for 15 minutes longer or until the popovers are brown and fully puffed.
- Remove immediately to a wire rack to prevent the popovers from becoming soggy.
- Pierce each popover with a knife to release the steam. Serve immediately or reheat just before serving.

Makes 1 dozen

Note: *Popovers are delicious filled with your favorite chicken salad.*

Wee Bread

    1/2   cup (1 stick) butter, softened
    1   cup sour cream, at room temperature
    1   cup self-rising flour, at room temperature

- Combine the butter and sour cream in a bowl and mix well. Blend in the self-rising flour just before baking.
- Fill lightly greased miniature muffin cups with the batter.
- Bake at 400 degrees for 15 minutes. Serve immediately.

Makes 2 dozen

Surf Puppies

    3   cups white cornmeal
    1/2   cup all-purpose flour
    3   tablespoons baking powder
    1 1/2 teaspoons salt
         Pinch of cayenne pepper
    1 1/2 cups well-shaken buttermilk
    4   eggs, lightly beaten
    1   cup minced onion
    2   garlic cloves, minced
         Vegetable oil for frying

- Combine the cornmeal, flour, baking powder, salt and cayenne pepper in a bowl and mix well. Add the buttermilk and eggs and mix well. Stir in the onion and garlic.
- Let the batter stand for 15 minutes.
- Drop the batter by heaping tablespoonfuls into hot oil in a deep skillet and fry for 3 minutes or until brown on all sides; drain. Serve immediately.

Makes 3 dozen

Pimento Corn Sticks

1	cup cornmeal	1	(4-ounce) jar chopped
1/3	cup all-purpose flour		pimentos, drained
4	teaspoons baking powder	1	cup sour cream
1	teaspoon salt	1/2	cup vegetable oil
1	(8-ounce) can	2	eggs, beaten
	cream-style corn	1/2	teaspoon baking soda

- Combine the cornmeal, flour, baking powder and salt in a bowl and mix well.
- Mix the corn, pimentos, sour cream, oil, eggs and baking soda in a bowl; stir into the cornmeal mixture.
- Heat the greased corn stick pans in 400-degree oven for 2 to 3 minutes.
- Spoon the batter into the hot pan and bake for 15 to 20 minutes or until light brown and crisp. Serve immediately.

Makes 16

Note: Can also be made into muffins.

Johnny Cakes

1	cup cornmeal	1	cup (4 ounces) shredded
1	teaspoon baking soda		Muenster cheese
1/2	teaspoon salt	1	cup cream-style corn
2	jalapeño chiles, seeded and	1/2	cup well-shaken buttermilk
	finely chopped	1/4	cup (1/2 stick) butter, melted
2	scallions, finely chopped	2	eggs, beaten

- Combine the cornmeal, baking soda and salt in a bowl and mix well. Stir in the jalapeño chiles and scallions.
- Mix the cheese, corn, buttermilk, butter and eggs in a bowl and stir into the cornmeal mixture just until moistened.
- Drop the batter by heaping tablespoonfuls onto a hot griddle. Cook until bubbles appear on the surface and the underside is brown; flip. Cook until brown on the remaining side. Serve immediately.

Serves 8

Note: Prepare small cakes as an appetizer and top with sour cream.

Sweet Pepper Jack Beer Bread

3 cups self-rising flour
1/2 cup sugar
1 cup (4 ounces) shredded Monterey Pepper Jack cheese or Cheddar cheese

1 (12-ounce) bottle beer
2 tablespoons chopped fresh chives (optional)
1/4 cup (1/2 stick) butter, melted

- Mix the self-rising flour, sugar and cheese in a bowl. Stir in the beer and chives.
- Spoon the batter into a lightly greased 5×9-inch loaf pan.
- Bake at 350 degrees for 45 minutes. Pour the butter over the top of the loaf and bake for 10 minutes longer.
- Cool in the pan for 10 minutes and remove to a wire rack.

Makes 1 loaf

Note: *To make a beer bread gift kit, place self-rising flour and sugar in a sealable plastic bag and tie the bag and recipe to a bottle of beer.*

Beaten Biscuits

3 cups all-purpose flour
1 teaspoon sugar
1/2 teaspoon salt
1/2 teaspoon baking powder

1/3 cup shortening or lard
1/4 cup ice water
1/4 cup milk

- Combine the flour, sugar, salt and baking powder in a food processor fitted with a chopping blade. Add the shortening and process just until crumbly.
- Add the ice water and milk gradually, processing constantly until the mixture forms a ball. Continue to process until the dough is smooth and elastic and slightly blistered.
- Roll the dough 1/2 inch thick on a lightly floured surface and cut into rounds with a 2-inch biscuit cutter.
- Arrange the rounds 1 inch apart on a greased baking sheet. Using a fork, pierce each round twice in a parallel row.
- Bake at 350 degrees for 30 to 35 minutes or until the tops start to brown and the undersides are golden brown. Serve warm.

Makes 1 1/2 dozen

Club Soda Biscuits

5   cups biscuit baking mix
1   cup sour cream
2/3 cup club soda
1/4 cup (1/2 stick) butter

- Combine the biscuit baking mix, sour cream and club soda in a bowl and mix well.
- Roll the dough on a lightly floured surface and cut into rounds using a biscuit cutter.
- Melt the butter in a 10×15-inch baking pan and tilt the pan to ensure even coverage. Arrange the rounds in a single layer in the prepared baking pan and bake at 375 degrees for 10 minutes or until golden brown. Serve immediately.
- Add herbs such as dill weed, rosemary, or thyme for a twist.

Makes 3 dozen

Note: *Use biscuit baking mix, not Bisquick.*

Cheddar Scallion Drop Biscuits

2 1/4 cups all-purpose flour
2 1/2 teaspoons baking powder
2   teaspoons sugar
1   teaspoon salt
3/4 teaspoon baking soda
6   tablespoons butter, cut into 1/2-inch cubes
1 1/2 cups (6 ounces) Cheddar cheese, coarsely shredded
3   scallions, finely chopped
1   cup well-shaken buttermilk

- Whisk the flour, baking powder, sugar, salt and baking soda in a bowl until combined. Cut in the butter until crumbly.
- Add the cheese and scallions. Stir in the buttermilk just until combined.
- Drop the dough in twenty-four equal mounds 2 inches apart onto a buttered baking sheet.
- Bake at 425 degrees on the middle oven rack for 15 to 18 minutes or until golden brown. Serve warm.

Makes 2 dozen

Note: *These are great served with ham.*

Park City French Bread

1	loaf French bread	2	tablespoons red wine
4	cups (16 ounces) shredded sharp Cheddar cheese	4	garlic cloves, minced
			Parsley to taste
1	cup (2 sticks) butter, softened		Paprika to taste

- Cut the loaf diagonally into twelve slices.
- Blend the cheese and butter in a bowl and stir in the wine and garlic.
- Spread the cheese mixture over one side of each slice of bread and sprinkle with parsley and paprika.
- Arrange the slices cheese side up on a baking sheet and broil until brown and bubbly. Serve immediately.

Makes 1 dozen slices

Three-Cheese Tomato Garlic Bread

1	loaf French bread	1/2	cup (2 ounces) shredded sharp provolone cheese
2	garlic cloves		
1	very ripe tomato, cut into halves	1/4	cup freshly grated Parmesan cheese
1	cup crumbled feta cheese	1	teaspoon minced rosemary

- Cut the loaf horizontally into lengthwise halves.
- Arrange the halves cut sides down on a grill rack and grill until lightly toasted.
- Rub the cut sides with the garlic cloves. Rub one tomato half over both toasted bread halves to cover with tomato juice. Chop the remaining tomato half and sprinkle evenly over the bread halves.
- Sprinkle the feta cheese, provolone cheese, Parmesan cheese and rosemary over the tomato.
- Wrap each half in foil and arrange on the grill rack toward the outer edge of the grill. Grill for 10 to 15 minutes or until the cheese melts. Cut each into 12 slices.
- May place on baking sheet and bake at 350 degrees for 10 minutes. Remove the foil and bake for 5 minutes longer.

Makes 2 dozen slices

March Madness

March equals basketball madness with the ACC tournament in southeastern North Carolina. While everyone is glued to the big screen, watching game after game, why not enjoy a party at home?

ACC Reuben Dip
Vegetable Mold

Elwood's Ham Chowder
Drunken Chili
It's Not Just Pimento Cheese sandwiches
Jalapeño Corn Bread Bites
Mixed greens with Garlic Vinaigrette

Chocolate Bread Pudding with Whiskey Sauce

Utagawa Hiroshige (Japanese, 1797–1885)
Station 3 Kawasaki (From the Fifty-Three Stations of the Tōkaidō), c.1855
Woodblock print, Publisher: Tsutaya, Format: oban tateye
Gift of Dr. Isabel Bittinger

Salads

The Cook's Canvas 2

Lemon Beef and Spinach Salad

3   lemons, sliced
1   (1½-pound) boneless sirloin steak, 1½ inches thick
8   cups baby spinach
    Garlic Vinaigrette (*page 109*)
    Freshly grated Parmigiano-Reggiano cheese or
    Parmesan cheese to taste

■   Arrange half the lemon slices in a single layer on a platter and top with the steak. Cover with the remaining lemon slices.

■   Wrap the platter in plastic wrap and let the steak stand at room temperature for 2 hours. Discard the lemons.

■   Grill the steak to the desired degree of doneness.

■   Toss the spinach with the Garlic Vinaigrette in a bowl. Add Parmigiano-Reggiano or Parmesan cheese and toss to mix. Thinly slice the steak and arrange over the spinach.

Serves 4

Chicken and Spinach Salad with Pearl Couscous

2 yellow onions, minced
2 tablespoons olive oil
2 teaspoons brown sugar
1 teaspoon dried basil
1 teaspoon dried thyme
1/4 teaspoon (or more) ground cinnamon
Salt and freshly ground pepper to taste
20 ounces dried apricots, diced
1 (12-ounce) package pearl couscous
4 cups chicken stock
2 cups bread crumbs
1/2 cup pistachios, finely chopped
6 boneless skinless chicken breasts
Olive oil for sautéing
12 ounces fresh baby spinach
1/4 cup chopped pistachios
Lemon Vinaigrette (*page 109*)

- Combine the onions, 2 tablespoons olive oil, the brown sugar, basil, thyme, cinnamon, salt and pepper in a baking dish and mix well. Bake at 350 degrees for 30 minutes or until the onions are tender.

- Stir the apricots into the onion mixture and bake for 20 minutes longer. Let stand until cool. Maintain the oven temperature.

- Cook the couscous according to the package directions, using stock for the liquid. Stir in the apricot mixture. Cover to keep warm.

- Mix the bread crumbs and 1/2 cup pistachios in a shallow dish. Coat the chicken with the bread crumb mixture.

- Sauté the chicken in olive oil in a skillet until brown on both sides, turning once. Remove the chicken to a baking pan. Bake for 45 minutes. Cool slightly and cut into thin slices.

- Line a serving platter with the spinach. Top with the warm couscous and sliced chicken. Sprinkle with 1/4 cup pistachios and drizzle with the desired amount of the Lemon Vinaigrette. Serve the remaining vinaigrette on the side.

Serves 8

Note: The spinach can be cooked and topped with chilled couscous and sliced warm chicken. Serve the vinaigrette on the side. Apricot couscous can be served hot or chilled as a side dish.

Lime Chicken Salad

1   cup mayonnaise
1/2 cup chutney
1/4 cup fresh lime juice
1   teaspoon curry powder
1   teaspoon grated lime zest
5   cups shredded cooked chicken or turkey breast
1/2 cup chopped fresh pineapple
1/2 cup sliced green onions
1/2 cup chopped celery
     Lettuce leaves
1/2 cup slivered almonds, toasted

- Combine the mayonnaise, chutney, lime juice, curry powder and lime zest in a large bowl and mix well. Fold in the chicken, pineapple, green onions and celery; chill, covered, in the refrigerator.
- Line a serving platter with lettuce leaves and top with the chicken salad. Sprinkle with the almonds and serve immediately.

Serves 6 to 8

Note: *Won Ton Cups are a wonderful way to serve salads or dips. Cut one won ton wrapper into four squares. Brush lightly with vegetable oil. Press oil side down into miniature muffin cups and bake at 350 degrees for about 10 minutes or until brown and crisp. Let stand until cool and fill with salads or dips just before serving.*

Grilled Shrimp Salad with Shoji Dressing

Shoji Dressing (*below*)

16 large shrimp, peeled and deveined

4 bamboo skewers
Olive oil

6 cups mixed salad greens with arugula

2 avocados, sliced
Sections of 2 oranges

1/2 red onion, thinly sliced
Toasted coconut or toasted sesame seeds

- Pour enough of the Shoji Dressing over the shrimp in a shallow dish to coat. Marinate, covered, in the refrigerator for several hours, turning occasionally.

- Soak the bamboo skewers in warm water for 15 minutes. Thread the shrimp onto the soaked skewers and brush lightly with olive oil.

- Grill over hot coals for 3 to 4 minutes or until the shrimp turn pink, turning after 2 minutes.

- Divide the salad greens evenly among four plates. Arrange the avocado slices, orange sections and onion slices over the greens. Top each serving with the shrimp from one skewer. Sprinkle with toasted coconut or sesame seeds and drizzle with the desired amount of the remaining dressing.

Serves 4

Shoji Dressing

1 1/2 cups olive oil

10 tablespoons minced onion

6 tablespoons rice vinegar

7 teaspoons soy sauce

7 teaspoons ketchup

7 teaspoons water

2 tablespoons minced celery

4 teaspoons minced fresh ginger

4 teaspoons finely grated lemon zest

1 teaspoon salt

1 teaspoon freshly ground pepper

- Combine the olive oil, onion, vinegar, soy sauce, ketchup, water, celery, ginger, lemon zest, salt and pepper in a food processor.

- Process until smooth. Store, covered, in the refrigerator.

Makes 3 cups

Note: Also serve on fruit salad with avocado, topped with toasted nuts.

Tomatoes Stuffed with Shrimp Salad

1¹/2 pounds shrimp
    Salt to taste
1   cup mayonnaise
8   gherkins, chopped
2   ribs celery, chopped
1   tablespoon chopped fresh tarragon
1   tablespoon chopped shallots
1   tablespoon chopped parsley
1   to 2 teaspoons Dijon mustard
1   hard-cooked egg, chopped (optional)
1   garlic clove, chopped (optional)
    Freshly ground pepper to taste
4   large tomatoes
    Sprigs of parsley
    Sprigs of tarragon

- Poach the shrimp in lightly salted water to cover in a large saucepan for 2 to 4 minutes or just until shrimp turn pink; drain. Do not overcook or shrimp will become tough.

- Peel, devein and coarsely chop the shrimp. Chill, covered, until cool.

- Combine the mayonnaise, gherkins, celery, chopped tarragon, shallots, chopped parsley and Dijon mustard in a bowl; mix well.

- Stir in the egg, garlic, salt and pepper. Add the shrimp and mix well. Chill, covered, until serving time.

- Cut each tomato into wedges to within ¹/2 inch of the bottom and fan out.

- Fill each tomato with one-fourth of the shrimp salad. Garnish with sprigs of parsley and sprigs of tarragon.

Serves 4

Note: Make your winter tomatoes taste like summer ones by placing them in a sunny windowsill for one or two days. Never store tomatoes in the refrigerator.

Marinated Shrimp and Crab Salad

2   pounds large shrimp, cooked, peeled and deveined
1   pound lump crab meat (*see Note page 22*)
1   pound fresh mushrooms, sliced
1   (14-ounce) can hearts of palm, drained and sliced
1   (8-ounce) can sliced water chestnuts, drained
8   ounces fresh or frozen snow peas
1   red bell pepper, julienned
     Seafood Marinade (*below*)
     Lettuce leaves

- Combine the shrimp, crab meat, mushrooms, hearts of palm, water chestnuts, snow peas and bell pepper in a shallow dish.
- Pour the Seafood Marinade over the shrimp mixture and toss gently.
- Marinate, covered, in the refrigerator for 8 to 10 hours or overnight to allow the flavors to blend, stirring occasionally.
- Drain and spoon the salad onto a lettuce-lined serving platter.

Serves 12 to 15

Seafood Marinade

1 1/2 cups white wine vinegar
3/4 cup olive oil
1/4 cup lemon juice
1/4 cup sugar
2 tablespoons chopped parsley

2 teaspoons lemon pepper
1 teaspoon dry mustard
1 teaspoon thyme
1 teaspoon basil
  Dash of hot red pepper sauce

- Whisk the vinegar, olive oil, lemon juice and sugar in a bowl until the sugar dissolves.
- Stir in the parsley, lemon pepper, dry mustard, thyme, basil and hot sauce.

Makes 2 1/2 cups

Grilled Tuna Salad with Asian Sesame Dressing

5 ounces organic mixed salad greens	Salt to taste
1/2 cup slivered almonds, toasted	Freshly ground pepper to taste
4 green onions, chopped	Asian Sesame Dressing (*below*)
Sections of 2 navel oranges	4 tuna fillets, grilled
	Rice noodles

- Toss the salad greens, almonds, green onions, oranges, salt and pepper with the desired amount of the Asian Sesame Dressing in a large bowl. Divide the salad evenly among four plates.
- Top each salad with one tuna fillet and sprinkle with rice noodles.
- Serve with the remaining dressing.

Serves 4

Asian Sesame Dressing

1/3 cup sugar	1 teaspoon lime juice
1/3 cup white wine vinegar or rice vinegar	1/4 teaspoon red pepper flakes
1/3 cup olive oil	1/4 teaspoon grated fresh ginger
1/4 cup sesame seeds, toasted	1/4 teaspoon toasted sesame oil

- Combine the sugar, vinegar, olive oil, sesame seeds, lime juice, red pepper flakes, ginger and sesame oil in a jar with a tight-fitting lid and seal tightly.
- Shake until the sugar dissolves and dressing is well mixed.

Makes 1 cup

Egg and Celery Salad

10   hard-cooked eggs
1/2 cup mayonnaise
1   tablespoon wine vinegar
1   tablespoon Dijon mustard
1¹/2 cups thinly sliced celery, blanched
     Salad greens
2   tablespoons finely chopped parsley

- Press two of the yolks through a sieve and set aside for garnish. Slice the remaining whole eggs and egg whites.
- Combine the mayonnaise, vinegar and Dijon mustard in a bowl and mix well. Fold in the sliced eggs, sliced egg whites and celery. Store, covered, in the refrigerator.
- Spoon the salad onto a platter lined with salad greens. Garnish with the reserved egg yolk and parsley.

Serves 8

Note: To prolong the life of celery, wrap in foil and store in the refrigerator. It will keep for weeks.

Wedge Salad with Green Goddess Dressing

1   head iceberg lettuce, sliced into 6 wedges and chilled Green Goddess Dressing (*below*)

2   cups cherry tomatoes, cut into halves

8   ounces bacon, crisp-cooked and crumbled

6   ounces blue cheese crumbles

- Arrange the lettuce wedges on individual salad plates.
- Drizzle with the Green Goddess Dressing and sprinkle with the tomatoes, bacon and cheese.
- Serve immediately.

Serves 6

Note: Iceberg lettuce, which is rinsed, dried, and wrapped in plastic wrap, will stay fresh and crisp for a long time in the refrigerator.

Green Goddess Dressing

1   cup mayonnaise

1/2   cup sour cream

3   tablespoons tarragon wine vinegar

2   tablespoons anchovy paste

1   teaspoon Worcestershire sauce

1/3   cup chopped fresh parsley

3   tablespoons minced fresh chives

1   large garlic clove, minced

1/2   teaspoon salt

1/2   teaspoon dry mustard

Freshly ground pepper to taste

- Combine the mayonnaise, sour cream, vinegar, anchovy paste and Worcestershire sauce in a bowl and mix well.
- Stir in the parsley, chives, garlic, salt, dry mustard and pepper.
- Store, covered, in the refrigerator.

Makes 2 cups

Note: If tarragon wine vinegar is not available, substitute with a mixture of 3 tablespoons white wine vinegar and 2 teaspoons dried tarragon.

Baby Greens Salad with Chèvre Cheese Toast

1/4 cup (1/2 stick) butter, softened
8 slices French bread baguette
8 ounces chèvre
1/4 cup chopped walnuts
1/4 cup finely chopped shallots
1/4 cup Grand Marnier
2 tablespoons balsamic vinegar
1 garlic clove, minced
3 tablespoons fresh orange juice

3 tablespoons Dijon mustard
1 tablespoon fresh lemon juice
1 teaspoon grated orange zest
Salt and freshly ground pepper to taste
1/2 cup extra-virgin olive oil
2 to 3 tablespoons walnut oil
12 ounces mixed baby salad greens
1/2 cup walnut pieces, toasted

- Spread the butter on the bread slices and arrange in a single layer on a baking sheet. Toast at 350 degrees until brown on both sides. Spread the chèvre on one side of each toast and sprinkle with the 1/4 cup walnuts.

- Combine the shallots, Grand Marnier, vinegar and garlic in a small saucepan and bring to a boil. Cook until reduced to 2 tablespoons, stirring occasionally.

- Combine the shallot reduction, orange juice, Dijon mustard, lemon juice, orange zest, salt and pepper in a bowl and mix well. Add the olive oil and walnut oil in a steady stream, whisking constantly until the mixture is emulsified.

- Arrange the cheese toasts on a baking sheet and broil 6 inches from the heat source for 1 minute.

- Combine the salad greens, 1/2 cup walnuts and shallot dressing in a bowl and toss to coat. Divide the salad evenly among serving plates and top each with two chèvre cheese toasts.

Serves 4

Note: Serve chèvre cheese toast with soups and other salads.

Harvest Cranberry Salad

9   slices smoked bacon
1/3 cup minced shallots
1   cup ruby port
1/2 cup dried cranberries
1   tablespoon balsamic vinegar
9   cups mixed salad greens
2   apples, sliced
4   ounces blue cheese, crumbled
1/2 cup walnuts, chopped

- Cook the bacon in a skillet until brown and crisp. Drain, reserving the drippings. Crumble the bacon.

- Spoon 3 tablespoons of the drippings into a bowl. Discard the remaining drippings, reserving 1 teaspoon in skillet.

- Add the shallots to the skillet and sauté over medium-high heat for 3 minutes or until tender. Stir in the port and cranberries.

- Bring to a boil, scraping any brown bits from the bottom of the skillet with a wooden spoon. Cook for 10 minutes or until the cranberries are tender and the liquid is reduced by half. Stir in the reserved 3 tablespoons bacon drippings. Cook just until heated through.

- Pour the vinegar into a small bowl and whisk in the cranberry mixture.

- Toss the salad greens with the cranberry dressing. Top with the bacon, apples, cheese and walnuts.

Serves 6

Note: The cranberry dressing may be prepared in advance and stored, covered, in the refrigerator. Reheat in the microwave. To prolong the life of salad greens, rinse, tear into bite-size pieces, dry in a salad spinner, and store in the spinner in the refrigerator until ready to use.

Watercress and Orange Salad with Walnut Vinaigrette

1/2 cup walnut oil
1/4 cup red wine vinegar
1/4 cup chopped
    walnuts, toasted
    Salt to taste

3 bunches watercress or baby
    spinach, trimmed and torn
    Sections of 3 oranges
    Thinly sliced red onion
    (optional)

■ Combine the walnut oil, vinegar, walnuts and salt in a jar and seal tightly. Shake to mix.

■ Combine the watercress or spinach, oranges and onion in a salad bowl. Add the vinaigrette and toss to coat.

Serves 6

Note: Toast nuts in the microwave for about 3 minutes.

Dunleigh Salad

3/4 cup olive oil
1/2 cup rice wine vinegar
1/2 cup chopped pecans or
    walnuts, toasted
1/2 cup golden raisins

1 bunch red leaf lettuce,
    trimmed and torn
1 cup (4 ounces) julienned
    Swiss cheese
    Julienned Virginia ham
    to taste

■ Whisk the olive oil and vinegar in a bowl until combined. Stir in the pecans and raisins.

■ Let stand at room temperature for 1 hour.

■ Arrange the lettuce in a crystal bowl. Layer the cheese and ham on top. Add the vinaigrette and toss until coated.

Serves 6

Note: Serve with Roasted Shallot and Smoked Bacon Soup (page 62).

Belgian Endive Salad with Smoked Bacon

6   heads Belgian endive
12   slices smoked bacon, crisp-cooked and crumbled
3/4   cup chopped tomato, drained
1/3   cup crumbled feta cheese
1/4   cup walnut pieces
2   tablespoons finely chopped fresh basil
    Balsamic Vinaigrette (*below*)

- Slice the root bottom off the endive. Separate into spears and tear into bite-size pieces.
- Combine the endive, bacon, tomato, cheese, walnuts and basil in a bowl.
- Add the Balsamic Vinaigrette and toss until coated.

Serves 6 to 8

Note: *Guests will be asking you for this recipe.*

Balsamic Vinaigrette

3   tablespoons balsamic vinegar
1   teaspoon Dijon mustard
1/2   cup olive oil
1   garlic clove, minced
1/4   teaspoon thyme
    Salt and freshly ground pepper to taste

- Whisk the vinegar and Dijon mustard in a bowl until combined. Add the olive oil gradually, whisking constantly until the olive oil is incorporated.
- Whisk in the garlic, thyme, salt and pepper.

Makes 3/4 cup

Note: *Do not overlook this versatile salad dressing, which is good on both pasta salads and mixed green salads.*

Wilted Spinach and Country Ham Salad with Candy Apple Vinaigrette

4   ounces country ham, chopped
8   ounces fresh spinach, stems removed
      Freshly ground pepper to taste
1/2   cup pecans, toasted
      Candy Apple Vinaigrette (*below*)

■   Cook the ham in a large skillet until the fat is rendered. Add the spinach and cook until slightly wilted.

■   Divide the spinach mixture evenly among four plates and sprinkle with pepper.

■   Top with the pecans and serve with the Candy Apple Vinaigrette on the side.

Serves 4

Candy Apple Vinaigrette

1/2   cup sugar
      Juice of 1 lemon
1   cup fresh cider or apple juice
1   cup cider vinegar
1/4   teaspoon freshly ground pepper
3   green apples, peeled and chopped into 1/2-inch pieces
1   tablespoon chopped shallots
2   tablespoons chopped fresh herbs (chives, basil, parsley, thyme or mint)
      Salt and freshly ground pepper to taste
3/4   cup olive oil

■   Mix the sugar and lemon juice in a saucepan. Cook over medium heat for 3 to 4 minutes or until caramel colored, stirring frequently.

■   Stir in the cider, vinegar and pepper and simmer for 5 to 8 minutes or until reduced by half. Add the apples, shallots, herbs, salt and pepper and mix well.

■   Cook over low heat until the apples are tender, stirring occasionally. Whisk in the olive oil until combined and let stand until cool.

Makes about 41/2 cups

South-of-the-Border Black Bean Salad

3	(15-ounce) cans black beans, drained and rinsed
2	(11-ounce) cans Mexicorn, drained
1	cup chopped fresh tomato
1	red bell pepper, chopped
1	yellow bell pepper, chopped
3/4	cup blanched slivered almonds, toasted
1/2	cup thinly sliced red onion or Vidalia onion
1/3	cup chopped cilantro
	Chili Garlic Vinaigrette (*below*)
	Salt and freshly ground pepper to taste
1	cup chopped ripe avocado

■ Combine the beans, corn, tomato, bell peppers, almonds, onion and cilantro in a bowl and mix well.

■ Add the Chili Garlic Vinaigrette and toss until coated. Season with salt and pepper.

■ Chill, covered, in the refrigerator. Add the avocado just before serving.

Serves 8

Chili Garlic Vinaigrette

1/2	cup balsamic vinegar
1/4	cup olive oil
1	garlic clove, minced
1	teaspoon chili powder
1/2	teaspoon ground cumin

■ Combine the vinegar, olive oil, garlic, chili powder and cumin in a bowl.

■ Whisk until combined.

Makes 3/4 cup

Note: Can also be used as a marinade.

Oriental Bean Sprouts with Sesame Dressing

3   cups mung bean sprouts, rinsed and dried
1 1/2 cups shredded carrots
1/2 cup shredded red bell pepper
4   scallions, cut into thin 3-inch-long strips
      Sesame Dressing (*below*)

- Heat a wok or sauté pan over high heat for 2 minutes.
- Spread the bean sprouts over the bottom of the hot wok. Cook the bean sprouts for 1 1/2 to 2 minutes or until brown, shaking the wok occasionally to avoid sticking.
- Turn the bean sprouts and brown on the remaining side. Remove the bean sprouts to a platter to cool.
- Combine the carrots, bell pepper and scallions in a salad bowl. Add the cooled bean sprouts and toss to mix.
- Add the Sesame Dressing and mix until coated. Serve immediately.

Serves 4

Sesame Dressing

3   tablespoons soy sauce
3   tablespoons red wine vinegar
1 1/2 tablespoons peanut oil
1 1/2 tablespoons sesame oil
2   teaspoons sugar
1   teaspoon minced garlic
1/2 teaspoon hot red pepper sauce

- Combine the soy sauce, vinegar, peanut oil, sesame oil, sugar, garlic and hot sauce in a jar with a tight-fitting lid and seal tightly.
- Shake to mix.
- Store in the refrigerator indefinitely.

Makes 1/2 cup

Lima Bean Salad

2 small sweet onions, chopped	1/2 teaspoon salt
1/2 cup olive oil	2 (15-ounce) cans lima beans,
1/4 cup lemon juice	drained
1 teaspoon hot sauce	Pimento strips

- Combine the onions, olive oil, lemon juice, hot sauce and salt in a bowl and mix well. Add the beans and toss until coated.
- Chill, covered, for 2 hours or longer. Garnish with pimento strips.

Serves 4

Note: This quick and easy salad goes well with boiled shrimp, or serve as an appetizer with crackers.

Crunchy Pea Salad

1 1/2 cups sour cream	8 ounces dry roasted peanuts
2 tablespoons soy sauce	2 (4-ounce) cans water
2 teaspoons toasted sesame oil	chestnuts, drained
1 teaspoon freshly ground	and chopped
pepper	1/2 bunch celery, trimmed and
4 (9-ounce) packages frozen	finely chopped
early or baby peas, thawed	2 large scallions, finely chopped
and drained	

- Whisk the sour cream, soy sauce, sesame oil and pepper in a bowl until combined.
- Combine the peas, peanuts, water chestnuts, celery and scallions in a bowl and mix well. Add the sour cream mixture and mix until coated.
- Chill, covered, for 2 to 10 hours.

Serves 8

Note: Very good and different.

Mediterranean Miniature Pepper Salad

1/2　cup balsamic vinegar
3　tablespoons extra-virgin
　　olive oil
3　garlic cloves, thinly sliced
1　teaspoon seasoned salt
1/2　teaspoon coarsely
　　ground pepper

3　cups sliced miniature
　　bell peppers
1　(15-ounce) can garbanzo
　　beans, drained and rinsed
1　(6-ounce) can pitted small
　　black olives, drained
1/2　cup crumbled feta cheese

■　Combine the vinegar, 2 tablespoons of the olive oil, garlic, salt and pepper in a bowl and mix well. Add the bell peppers and stir until coated. Marinate in the refrigerator for 8 to 10 hours, stirring occasionally. Drain, reserving the marinade.

■　Mix the remaining 1 tablespoon olive oil and 2 tablespoons of the reserved marinade in a bowl. Add additional marinade if desired for a more vinegary flavor. Stir in the marinated bell peppers, beans and olives.

■　Store, covered, in the refrigerator for up to 2 days. Toss with the feta cheese just before serving.

Serves 4 to 6

Marinated Potato Salad

2　pounds unpeeled red potatoes,
　　cut into bite-size pieces
6　tablespoons red or white
　　wine vinegar
1　shallot or 1/2 red onion,
　　chopped, or 3 tablespoons
　　minced chives
2　tablespoons minced parsley

2　tablespoons drained capers
1　tablespoon whole grain or
　　Dijon mustard
1　tablespoon (or more) fresh
　　minced tarragon, mint,
　　dill weed, or thyme (optional)
6　tablespoons olive oil

■　Place the potatoes in enough cold water to cover in a saucepan and bring to a boil. Reduce the heat and cook until the potatoes are tender; drain.

■　Whisk the vinegar, shallot, parsley, capers, whole grain mustard and tarragon in a bowl until combined. Add the olive oil gradually, whisking until incorporated.

■　Pour the dressing over the warm potatoes and toss gently. Serve at room temperature or chilled.

Serves 8

Coleslaw

3	pounds cabbage, trimmed	2	cups sugar
2	green bell peppers, seeded	2	cups vinegar
3	onions, cut into wedges	1	tablespoon salt
1	(4-ounce) jar chopped	1	tablespoon mustard seeds
	pimentos, drained	1	tablespoon prepared
2	cups water		horseradish

- Pulse the cabbage, bell peppers and onions separately in a food processor until ground. Spoon the vegetables into a bowl and stir in the pimentos.
- Combine the water, sugar, vinegar, salt, mustard seeds and horseradish in a saucepan and mix well. Cook until heated through, stirring frequently. Let stand until cool. Pour the vinegar dressing over the cabbage mixture and toss until coated.

Serves 12

Note: Store indefinitely in the refrigerator.

Oriental Cucumber and Bell Pepper Slaw

2	English cucumbers, or 4 cucumbers, thinly sliced	2	bunches radishes, trimmed and sliced
2	green bell peppers, thinly sliced	6	tablespoons vegetable oil
		1/4	cup rice vinegar
2	red bell peppers, thinly sliced	2	tablespoons sugar
1	yellow bell pepper, thinly sliced	1	teaspoon soy sauce
			Salt to taste
2	cups fresh bean sprouts	2	heads Boston lettuce, separated into leaves
1	Vidalia onion, thinly sliced		

- Combine the cucumbers, bell peppers, bean sprouts, onion and radishes in a bowl and mix well. Chill, covered, in the refrigerator.
- Combine the oil, vinegar, sugar, soy sauce and salt in a jar with a tight-fitting lid and seal tightly. Shake to mix. Pour over the chilled cucumber mixture just before serving and mix well. Spoon the salad onto a lettuce-lined platter.

Serves 6 to 8

Note: The range of brilliant colors of the vegetables makes this a beautiful salad.

Orange Couscous Salad

2 cups water
1/2 teaspoon salt
1 1/2 cups couscous
1 cup julienned carrots, steamed
1 cup julienned green beans, steamed
1 large red bell pepper, julienned
1/2 cup slivered almonds, toasted
1/3 cup chopped red onion
1/3 cup raisins
Citrus Dressing (*below*)

■ Bring the water and salt to a boil in a saucepan and stir in the couscous. Remove from the heat and let stand, covered, until the liquid is absorbed. Remove the cover and let stand until cool.

■ Combine the couscous, carrots, beans, bell pepper, almonds, onion and raisins in a bowl and mix well.

■ Add the Citrus Dressing and toss to coat.

Serves 8

Citrus Dressing

1/2 cup olive oil
1/4 cup lemon juice
1/4 cup chopped fresh parsley
3 tablespoons orange juice
1 tablespoon chopped fresh mint
1/4 teaspoon ground cinnamon
Cayenne pepper to taste

■ Combine the olive oil, lemon juice, parsley, orange juice, mint, cinnamon and cayenne pepper in a jar with a tight-fitting lid and seal tightly. Shake to mix.

Makes 1 1/4 cups

Note: Colorful, light, and refreshing.

Rice Salad

3   cups cooked rice, chilled
1   cup green peas
1/2 cup chopped chutney
1/2 cup chopped celery
1   tablespoon finely chopped onion
1/2 cup chopped parsley
2/3 cup mayonnaise
1   tablespoon vegetable oil
1   tablespoon wine vinegar
     Salt and freshly ground pepper to taste

- Combine the rice, peas, chutney, celery, onion and parsley in a bowl and mix well.
- Mix the mayonnaise, oil and vinegar in a bowl until blended. Stir into the rice mixture. Season with salt and pepper.
- Chill, covered, until serving time.

Serves 6 to 8

Note: Chopped chicken or ham may be added for a heartier salad. To make a ring mold, coat the inside of a mold with oil or mayonnaise and lightly pat the rice mixture into the prepared mold. Chill, covered, in the refrigerator. Invert onto a serving platter just before serving.

Dried Cherry Orzo Salad with Orange Vinaigrette

6 cups water
1 tablespoon salt
3/4 cup orzo
1/2 cup chopped dried cherries
1/2 cup finely chopped celery
1/4 cup chopped sweet onion

2 tablespoons chopped parsley
1/4 teaspoon salt
Freshly ground pepper
to taste
Orange Vinaigrette (*below*)

■ Bring the water to a boil in a large saucepan and stir in 1 tablespoon salt. Return to a boil and stir in the pasta.

■ Cook for 5 to 7 minutes or just until al dente; drain.

■ Combine the pasta, cherries, celery, onion, parsley, 1/4 teaspoon salt and pepper in a bowl and mix well. Add the Orange Vinaigrette and toss until coated.

■ Adjust the seasonings to taste. Serve immediately or serve at room temperature.

Serves 4

Orange Vinaigrette

1 tablespoon grated orange zest
1 tablespoon orange juice
2 teaspoons white wine vinegar
1/4 teaspoon salt
1/4 teaspoon freshly ground
   pepper

2 tablespoons olive oil
Salt and freshly ground
pepper to taste

■ Combine the orange zest, orange juice, vinegar, 1/4 teaspoon salt and 1/4 teaspoon pepper in a bowl and mix well.

■ Whisk in the olive oil until blended.

■ Season with salt and pepper to taste.

Makes 1/4 cup

Note: *This dressing is also good on fruit salad.*

Sesame Noodles

16   ounces vermicelli pasta
6   tablespoons sunflower oil
2   tablespoons toasted sesame oil
6   garlic cloves, finely chopped
2   tablespoons finely chopped fresh ginger
6   tablespoons light-brewed rice vinegar
6   tablespoons soy sauce
3   tablespoons sugar
1   tablespoon Chinese hot oil or chili oil
6   scallions, chopped

- Cook the pasta using the package directions until al dente. Rinse with cold water and drain.
- Heat the sunflower oil and sesame oil in a saucepan until hot. Stir in the garlic and ginger.
- Sauté until tender but not brown. Stir in the vinegar, soy sauce, sugar and Chinese hot oil. Bring to a boil and boil for a few seconds. Toss with the pasta in a large bowl until coated.
- Chill, covered, for 24 hours. Toss the pasta several times and let stand until room temperature. Stir in the scallions.

Serves 8

Note: *Tangy Oriental flavors blend to perfection. Must be prepared one day in advance.*

Mykonos Pasta Salad

16 ounces acini di pepe pasta
4   Roma tomatoes, chopped
3   ribs celery, chopped
1   cucumber, peeled, seeded
    and chopped
5   green onions, chopped

2   small red or yellow bell
    peppers, chopped
12 ounces feta cheese, crumbled
    (about 3 cups)
20 Greek olives
10 pickled pepperoncini, minced
    Greek Dressing (*below*)

- Cook the pasta using the package directions until al dente; drain.
- Combine the pasta, tomatoes, celery, cucumber, green onions, bell peppers, cheese, olives and pepperoncini in a bowl and mix well.
- Add the Greek Dressing and toss to coat.
- Chill, covered, for 2 to 3 hours to allow the flavors to blend, stirring occasionally.

Serves 8

Note: *For a main course, add 4 sliced cooked chicken breasts or 2 pounds peeled and deveined cooked shrimp.*

Greek Dressing

6   tablespoons fresh lemon juice
1/4   cup red wine vinegar
4   garlic cloves, minced
3   tablespoons minced fresh oregano
1   teaspoon salt
1   teaspoon freshly ground pepper
2/3   cup extra-virgin olive oil
1 1/2 cups chopped fresh parsley

- Whisk the lemon juice, vinegar, garlic, oregano, salt and pepper in a bowl until combined.
- Add the olive oil gradually, whisking constantly until incorporated. Stir in the parsley.

Makes 3 1/2 cups

Note: *For best results use fresh herbs.*

Tortellini Salad with Sun-Dried Tomatoes

1   (9-ounce) package fresh
spinach cheese tortellini

1   (9-ounce) package fresh
mozzarella garlic tortellini
Dijon Vinaigrette (*below*)

2   cups shrimp

2   cups snow peas or
sugar snap peas

1   (6-ounce) can medium pitted
whole black olives, drained

1   (8-ounce) jar oil-pack sun-
dried tomatoes, drained and
cut in thirds

6   fresh basil leaves,
coarsely chopped

- Cook the pasta using the package directions; drain. Toss the pasta with a little of the Dijon Vinaigrette in a bowl. Chill, covered, in the refrigerator.
- Cook the shrimp in boiling water in a saucepan until the shrimp turn pink; drain. Peel and devein the shrimp. Chill, covered, in a bowl in the refrigerator.
- Combine the pasta, shrimp, snow peas, olives, sun-dried tomatoes and basil in a bowl. Add the remaining vinaigrette and toss until coated. Chill, covered, for 8 to 10 hours.

Serves 8

Note: For a great appetizer, drain the salad and alternately thread the ingredients on skewers.

Dijon Vinaigrette

2   tablespoons red wine vinegar

2   teaspoons Dijon mustard

1   teaspoon salt

2   garlic cloves, minced

1/2   teaspoon dried thyme, or
1 1/4 teaspoons chopped
fresh thyme

7   tablespoons olive oil

5   tablespoons vegetable oil

- Whisk the vinegar, Dijon mustard, salt, garlic and thyme in a bowl until combined.
- Add the olive oil and vegetable oil gradually, whisking constantly until the oils are incorporated.

Makes 1 cup

Note: Substitute 3 tablespoons sun-dried tomato oil for 3 tablespoons of the olive oil, if desired.

Gazpacho Aspic with Homemade Lemon Mayonnaise

3   envelopes unflavored gelatin
2¹/4 cups tomato juice
¹/3 cup red wine vinegar
1¹/2 teaspoons salt
¹/4 teaspoon hot red pepper sauce
1¹/2 cups chopped peeled
     tomatoes
1   large cucumber, peeled and
    chopped (1¹/2 cups)
1   green bell pepper, minced

¹/2 cup finely chopped onion
1   (2-ounce) jar chopped
    pimento, drained (optional)
¹/4 cup chopped green olives
1   garlic clove, minced
3   large ripe avocados
    Lemon juice
    Homemade Lemon
    Mayonnaise (*below*) or
    Basic Vinaigrette (*page 109*)

■ Soften the gelatin in half the tomato juice in a saucepan. Cook over low heat until the gelatin dissolves, stirring constantly. Stir in the remaining tomato juice, the vinegar, salt and hot sauce.

■ Chill for 30 minutes or until partially set. Stir in the tomatoes, cucumber, bell pepper, onion, pimento, olives and garlic. Pour the tomato mixture into a 2¹/2-quart mold and chill until set. Slice the avocados just before serving and drizzle with lemon juice. Unmold onto a decorative platter and arrange the sliced avocados around the aspic. Serve with the Homemade Lemon Mayonnaise or the Basic Vinaigrette.

Serves 8

Homemade Lemon Mayonnaise

1   tablespoon fresh lemon juice
2   teaspoons Worcestershire
    sauce
¹/2 teaspoon salt

¹/2 teaspoon dry mustard
    Dash of hot red pepper sauce
3   egg yolks
2   cups vegetable oil

■ Mix the lemon juice, Worcestershire sauce, salt, dry mustard and hot sauce in a bowl.

■ Place the egg yolks in a mixing bowl. Add the lemon juice mixture gradually, whisking constantly. Add the oil gradually, beating constantly until thickened. Store, covered, in the refrigerator.

Makes 1¹/2 cups

Note: If you are concerned about using raw egg yolks, use eggs pasteurized in their shells, which are sold at some specialty food stores, or use an equivalent amount of pasteurized egg substitute.

Grapefruit Salad

2   grapefruit
1   orange
1   lemon
3   envelopes unflavored gelatin
3/4 cup water
1/2 cup sugar
1/4 teaspoon salt
1   cup dry white wine
2   tablespoons lemon juice
1   cup seedless red grapes, cut into halves
1/2 cup slivered almonds, toasted
3   tablespoons julienned crystallized ginger (optional)
     Homemade Lemon Mayonnaise (*page 105*)

- Peel the grapefruit, orange and lemon over a sieve in a bowl to reserve the juices. Squeeze any remaining juice from the peels into the bowl. Add enough water to the juices to measure 2 1/2 cups.

- Cut the grapefruit, orange and lemon into sections.

- Soften the gelatin in 3/4 cup water in a bowl. Combine the softened gelatin, juice mixture, sugar and salt in a saucepan and heat until the gelatin dissolves, stirring constantly. Stir in the wine and lemon juice.

- Chill until partially set. Fold in the grapefruit, orange, lemon, grapes, almonds and ginger. Pour into a 1-quart mold or ten individual molds. Chill until set.

- Invert the mold onto a serving platter and serve with the Homemade Lemon Mayonnaise.

Serves 10

Note: May add finely chopped crystallized ginger to the mayonnaise.

Fruit Salad with Ginger Syrup

3   cups water
2   cups sugar
2   cups thinly sliced unpeeled fresh ginger (8 ounces)
8   cups fresh summer fruit (melon balls, blueberries,
      pineapple wedges, nectarine and orange sections)
      Finely chopped fresh mint
2   cups fresh red raspberries

- Combine the water, sugar and ginger in a saucepan and bring to a boil. Boil until the sugar dissolves, stirring constantly. Reduce the heat to low.
- Simmer for 20 to 30 minutes, stirring occasionally. Remove from the heat and let stand for 30 minutes.
- Strain the syrup through a sieve into a bowl, discarding the ginger. Chill, covered, for 2 hours or longer.
- Place the fresh fruit in a large glass bowl. Pour a small amount of the syrup over the fruit and toss gently. Chill, covered, for several hours.
- Pour the remaining syrup over the fruit 1 hour before serving and chill; drain. Add mint and toss gently to mix.
- Add the raspberries about 15 minutes before serving and mix gently.

Serves 10

Note: Before peeling oranges, cover with boiling water and let stand for 5 minutes. The bitter white membrane is then easily removed. Preserve peeled fresh ginger in a wide-mouth jar covered with good-quality dry sherry or vodka.

Flavored Oils

Rosemary Oil

Fresh rosemary leaves   Olive oil

- Lightly pack a jar with rosemary leaves and fill to the top with olive oil. Press the leaves down with a chopstick until no air bubbles remain and seal tightly.
- Store the jar in a dark, dry environment at room temperature for 2 to 3 weeks.
- Every 3 days open the jar and refill to the top with olive oil, breaking any air bubbles.
- Strain the oil through cheesecloth into a bowl, discarding the solids.
- Serve on roasted vegetables, especially potatoes. Or, add a few tablespoons to steamed green beans.

Herb-Flavored Oil

8   to 10 sprigs of fresh herb   1   bay leaf (optional)
    of choice   Olive oil
1   teaspoon peppercorns

- Place the herb sprigs, peppercorns and bay leaf in a bottle and add enough olive oil to cover tightly.
- Place the bottle in a sunny window for 1 week or longer, shaking periodically.
- A roasted chicken is delicious basted with tarragon oil.

Capers and Oil

1   (7-ounce) jar vinegar-pack   Sprigs of rosemary
    capers, drained   3   cups Olive oil

- Place the capers in a jar or bottle and add the rosemary. Fill to the top with the olive oil and seal tightly with a lid or cork.
- Place the jar in a sunny window for 1 week or longer, shaking periodically.
- Great on a summer tomato salad with basil and red onion.

Lemon Garlic Oil

$1/2$ lemon, cut into 3 slices
     and seeded

3   garlic cloves
     Olive oil

- Thread the lemon slices and garlic cloves alternately on a bamboo skewer.
- Place the skewer in a jar or bottle and fill with olive oil.
- Seal tightly with a cork and place the jar in a sunny window for 1 week or longer, shaking periodically.

Basic Vinaigrette

1   cup oil of choice, or
     combination of several oils

$1/3$ cup red wine vinegar or
     vinegar of choice

$1/4$ cup minced shallots

2   teaspoons Dijon mustard

$1 1/2$ teaspoons sugar

$1/2$ teaspoon salt
     Freshly ground pepper to taste

- Whisk the oil, vinegar, shallots, Dijon mustard, sugar, salt and pepper in a bowl until combined.
- Let stand for 2 to 3 hours to allow the flavors to blend.

Makes $1 1/2$ cups

Variations

Lemon Vinaigrette: *Substitute fresh lemon juice for the vinegar and honey for the sugar. Add 2 teaspoons grated lemon zest.*

Garlic Vinaigrette: *Add 1 or 2 minced garlic cloves and 1 tablespoon chopped fresh parsley.*

Herb Vinaigrette: *Add 1 to 2 tablespoons chopped fresh herbs such as chives, tarragon, mint, marjoram, basil, oregano and/or parsley.*

Dijon Vinaigrette: *Add 3 additional tablespoons Dijon mustard.*

Note: *For any of these vinaigrettes, you may use a blender to create a creamier dressing by partially emulsifying the oil and vinegar together.*

Lemon Tahini Dressing

1/3 cup lemon juice
1/4 cup water
1/4 cup tahini
1/4 cup tamari
1/2 teaspoon white pepper
1/4 cup chopped onion

2 tablespoons chopped green bell pepper
1 small rib celery, chopped
1/2 cup olive oil
1 tablespoon ponzu (optional)

- Combine the lemon juice, water, tahini, tamari and white pepper in a food processor fitted with a steel blade. Pulse until combined.
- Add the onion, bell pepper and celery and pulse until the vegetables are minced.
- Add the olive oil gradually, processing constantly until the olive oil is incorporated.
- Add the ponzu and process until blended. Store in the refrigerator.

Makes 1 3/4 cups

Roquefort Dressing

1 cup mayonnaise
6 tablespoons crumbled blue cheese
3 tablespoons crumbled Roquefort cheese
6 tablespoons buttermilk

2 tablespoons tarragon vinegar
1/2 teaspoon sugar
Pinch of garlic powder
1 to 2 teaspoons Worcestershire sauce
Salt to taste

- Combine the mayonnaise, blue cheese, Roquefort cheese, buttermilk, vinegar, sugar and garlic powder in a bowl and mix well.
- Add the Worcestershire sauce gradually, whisking constantly and tasting as you add. Season with salt.
- Store in an airtight container in the refrigerator.

Makes 2 1/4 cups

Note: This flavorful dressing can also be used as a dip.

Azalea Festival

No place celebrates spring better than Wilmington during its internationally renowned Azalea Festival. Public and private gardens are open to the public for viewing and snapping family portraits. Our city glows pink and purple for weeks with azalea blooms. Celebrate spring in your garden with a luncheon.

Cheese Wafers with Candied Ginger
Garden Party Onion Sandwiches
Vegetable Mold served on cucumbers
Lime Chicken Salad in won ton cups
New Orleans Shrimp
Ham biscuits with Cranberry Rum Relish
Rice Salad
Fruit Salad with Ginger Syrup

Marmalade Cake
Toasted Almond Pound Cake with Balsamic Strawberries

Attributed to Caroline Von Glahn (American, 1843–1903)
Untitled (River and Millhouse), n.d.
Pastel on paper
Gift of Katherine Von Glahn

Meat & Poultry

The Cook's Canvas 2

Garlic and Herb Crusted Beef Top Loin Roast

4   garlic cloves
8   fresh sage leaves
4   teaspoons chopped fresh thyme leaves
4   teaspoons olive oil
4   teaspoons salt
1 1/2 teaspoons freshly ground pepper
1   (2- to 3-pound) boneless top loin beef roast, trimmed

- Process the garlic in a food processor until finely chopped. Add the sage, thyme, olive oil, salt and pepper and process to make a paste.

- Pat the roast dry with paper towels and rub the paste over the surface of the roast. Chill, covered, for 3 to 24 hours.

- Place the roast fat side up on a rack in a roasting pan and roast at 450 degrees for 15 minutes. Reduce the oven temperature to 350 degrees.

- Roast for 35 minutes longer or until a meat thermometer inserted in the thickest portion of the roast registers 130 degrees for medium-rare or 140 degrees for medium.

- Let stand for 20 minutes and slice crosswise into 1/3-inch-thick slices.

Serves 4 to 6

Note: *Serve with Potato, Leek and Turnip au Gratin (page 181) and Grand Marnier Carrot Bundles (page 170).*

Marinated New York Strip Steak with Horseradish Sauce

4   (10- to 12-ounce) New York strip steaks
1/2 cup Worcestershire sauce
1   bay leaf
3/4 teaspoon olive oil
1/2 teaspoon dried thyme leaves
1/2 teaspoon dried rosemary leaves
1/2 teaspoon minced fresh garlic
    Horseradish Sauce (*below*)

- Arrange the steaks in a single layer in a large shallow dish.
- Mix the Worcestershire sauce, bay leaf, olive oil, thyme, rosemary and garlic in a bowl and pour over the steaks, turning to coat.
- Marinate, covered, in the refrigerator for 6 to 8 hours, turning occasionally. Remove from the marinade.
- Grill or broil the steaks to the desired degree of doneness and serve with the Horseradish Sauce.

Serves 4

Horseradish Sauce

1   cup sour cream
3   tablespoons prepared horseradish
2   teaspoons Worcestershire sauce
1/2 teaspoon salt

- Combine the sour cream, prepared horseradish, Worcestershire sauce and salt in a bowl and mix well.
- Store, covered, in the refrigerator.

Makes 1 1/4 cups

Beef Tenderloin

1   (4-pound) beef tenderloin, trimmed
     Salt and freshly ground pepper to taste

- Season the tenderloin with salt and pepper and place fat side up in a baking pan.
- Roast at 400 degrees until a meat thermometer registers 120 degrees for rare, 125 degrees for medium-rare or 140 degrees for medium.
- Remove the tenderloin from the oven and tent with foil.
- Let stand for 10 to 15 minutes before carving.

Serves 6 to 8

Variation: Marinate beef tenderloin or pork tenderloin in the refrigerator for several hours with a mixture of one bottle of Italian salad dressing, 6 minced garlic cloves and 1/4 cup Worcestershire sauce. Never pierce meat with a fork while roasting or grilling as this allows the juices to escape.

Prime Rib Roast

1	(12-pound) prime rib roast (about 5 ribs)	1	teaspoon garlic powder
		1	teaspoon ground thyme
1	teaspoon freshly ground pepper	1	teaspoon ground oregano
		1	teaspoon sage

- Let the roast stand at room temperature for about 1 hour.
- Combine the pepper, garlic powder, thyme, oregano and sage in a bowl and rub the mixture over the surface of the roast.
- Place the roast fat side up on a rack in a roasting pan.
- Roast at 375 degrees for 1 hour. Turn off the oven and let the roast stand in closed oven. Do not open the door.
- Turn the oven to 375 degrees 1 hour before serving. Do not open the door. Roast for 30 to 40 minutes longer for medium-rare.
- Let stand for 5 minutes before slicing.

Serves 12 to 16

Green Enchiladas

1 pound lean ground beef
1/2 cup chopped onion
1 garlic clove, minced
1 teaspoon salt
8 ounces Cheddar cheese, shredded
1 cup medium-hot salsa
1 (10-ounce) can cream of chicken soup
1 (5-ounce) can evaporated milk
1 (4-ounce) can chopped green chiles
8 ounces Monterey Jack cheese, shredded
6 to 8 (10-inch) tortillas

- Brown the ground beef with the onion and garlic in a skillet, stirring until the ground beef is crumbly; drain. Stir in the salt.
- Let stand until cool and stir in the Cheddar cheese and salsa.
- Combine the soup, evaporated milk, green chiles and Monterey Jack cheese in a saucepan. Cook over medium heat until the cheese melts, stirring frequently.
- Spoon 1/4 cup of the ground beef mixture down the center of each tortilla. Roll to enclose the filling and arrange seam side down in a 9×13-inch baking pan.
- Pour the soup mixture over the top and bake at 350 degrees for 30 minutes.

Serves 6

Note: A great addition to your "busy day" entertaining file, this takes 20 minutes to prepare.

Broiled Deviled Hamburgers

1   pound ground chuck
1/2 cup fine bread crumbs
1/4 cup dry red wine
3   tablespoons chili sauce
1   tablespoon minced onion
1   teaspoon Worcestershire sauce
1   teaspoon prepared mustard
1   teaspoon prepared horseradish
1   garlic clove, minced
1/4 teaspoon mace (optional)
    Salt and freshly ground pepper to taste
    Picadilla Sauce (optional) (*page 119*)
    Marinated Vidalia Onions (optional) (*page 119*)

- Combine the ground chuck, bread crumbs, wine, chili sauce, onion and Worcestershire sauce in a bowl and mix well.

- Add the prepared mustard, prepared horseradish, garlic, mace, salt and pepper; mix well.

- Shape the ground chuck mixture into six patties.

- Arrange the patties on a rack in a broiler pan. Broil for 3 minutes on each side for medium or 4 minutes on each side for well done.

- Serve with Picadilla Sauce or Marinated Vidalia Onions.

Serves 6

Picadilla Sauce

2	tablespoons olive oil	1	(4-ounce) can mild green
4	yellow, red or orange bell		chiles, drained and chopped
	peppers, finely chopped	1	teaspoon ground cumin
1	red onion, finely chopped	1	(7-ounce) jar pimento-stuffed
4	garlic cloves, finely chopped		green olives, finely chopped
2	(14-ounce) cans diced	1	(3-ounce) jar capers, drained
	tomatoes		

■ Heat the olive oil in a saucepan and stir in the bell peppers and onion. Sauté until tender. Add the garlic and sauté for 1 minute. Stir in the tomatoes, green chiles and cumin.

■ Simmer for 20 minutes, stirring occasionally. Add the olives and capers and simmer for 2 minutes longer. Serve hot or chilled. Freeze for future use if desired.

Makes 5 cups

Note: Serve with Broiled Deviled Hamburgers (page 118). Wonderful on meatloaf or chicken. The flavor is enhanced if prepared in advance and stored, covered, in the refrigerator. Reheat if desired before serving.

Marinated Vidalia Onions

1	cup vinegar	1/2	cup mayonnaise
1	cup sugar	1	teaspoon celery seeds
1	cup water	1	teaspoon celery salt
6	Vidalia onions, thinly sliced		

■ Mix the vinegar, sugar and water in a bowl and stir until the sugar dissolves. Add the onions. Marinate for 2 to 10 hours and drain.

■ Combine the mayonnaise, celery seeds and celery salt in a bowl and mix well. Add the onions; mix well. Chill, covered, until serving time.

Makes 1 1/2 cups

Note: Serve on Broiled Deviled Hamburgers (page 118), or as an appetizer with crackers.

Roasted Veal Shanks

8   (8-ounce) meaty veal shanks
     Salt and freshly ground pepper to taste
1/3   cup olive oil
2   carrots, finely chopped
1   onion, finely chopped
2   ribs celery, finely chopped
3   garlic cloves, finely chopped
3   tablespoons chopped parsley
2   tablespoons chopped fresh sage,
     or 1 tablespoon dried sage
2   tablespoons chopped fresh thyme,
     or 1/2 teaspoon dried thyme
1   cup dry white wine
1   tablespoon tomato paste

- Season the veal with salt and pepper. Brush the bottom of a baking dish with 2 tablespoons of the olive oil.

- Arrange the veal in a single layer with the wider part of the bone facing up in the prepared baking dish. Drizzle with the remaining olive oil.

- Roast at 350 degrees for 30 minutes. Remove the veal to a platter, reserving the pan drippings. Maintain the oven temperature.

- Add the carrots, onion, celery, garlic, parsley, sage and thyme to the reserved pan drippings and mix well. Season with salt and pepper.

- Arrange the veal over the vegetable mixture and pour 1/2 cup of the wine over the top. Roast for 15 minutes.

- Drizzle with the remaining 1/2 cup wine. Roast for 20 minutes, basting the veal with the pan drippings twice.

- Reduce the heat to 325 degrees and cover loosely with foil. Roast for 30 minutes longer or until the veal is tender. Remove the veal to a serving platter using a slotted spoon.

- Process the roasted vegetable mixture and tomato paste in a food processor fitted with a steel blade until puréed. Pour the purée over the veal and serve immediately.

Serves 8

Braised Lamb with Artichoke Hearts

1/2 cup dry white wine or vermouth
1 (6-ounce) can tomato paste
2 tablespoons wine vinegar
2 tablespoons currants
1 tablespoon honey
2 garlic cloves, minced
1 1/2 teaspoons dried thyme
3 pounds boneless lamb, trimmed and
    cut into 1 1/2-inch pieces
    Salt and freshly ground pepper to taste
1/4 cup olive oil
2 large onions, finely chopped (1 1/2 cups)
1 (8-ounce) package frozen artichoke hearts,
    thawed just to separate
6 tablespoons chopped fresh parsley

- Mix the wine, tomato paste, vinegar, currants, honey, garlic and thyme in a bowl.
- Season the lamb generously with salt and pepper.
- Heat the olive oil in a Dutch oven. Cook the lamb in batches in the oil until brown on all sides. Return the cooked lamb to the Dutch oven.
- Spread the onions over the lamb and pour the wine mixture over the top. Simmer, covered, for 2 hours; do not stir.
- Submerge the artichoke hearts in the pan juices. Simmer, covered, for 45 minutes longer or until the lamb and artichokes are tender.
- Gently stir in the parsley just before serving. Adjust salt and pepper to taste.

Serves 6

Note: *Freezes well.*

Grilled Marinated Leg of Lamb

1   (6-pound) leg of lamb, boned and butterflied
1   teaspoon coarsely cracked pepper
4   garlic cloves, sliced
1/2   cup red wine
1/2   cup olive oil
2   tablespoons vinegar
2   tablespoons salt
2   bay leaves
1/2   teaspoon dried tarragon

■ Spread the lamb flat in a glass dish. Sprinkle with the pepper and garlic.

■ Mix the wine, olive oil, vinegar, salt, bay leaves and tarragon in a bowl and pour over the lamb.

■ Marinate, covered, in the refrigerator for 24 hours, turning several times. Remove the lamb from the marinade.

■ Grill the lamb over low heat for 6 minutes per side or until crusty and brown. Spread the coals to reduce the heat further and continue to grill the lamb 6 minutes per side for a total of 24 minutes or to the desired degree of doneness.

■ Slice as you would a steak and serve.

Serves 8

Variation: For a different marinade, mix 1 cup cold strong coffee, 1/2 cup packed brown sugar, 1/2 cup lemon juice, 2 tablespoons prepared mustard, 1 teaspoon Worcestershire sauce, 2 minced garlic cloves and a dash of Tabasco sauce. Pour over the lamb and marinate in the refrigerator for 8 hours.

Pork Medallions with Green Peppercorn Sauce

1¹/2 pounds pork tenderloin, cut into
    1-inch-thick medallions
    Salt and freshly ground pepper to taste
3   tablespoons butter
4   shallots, chopped
1/2 cup dry vermouth
1¹/2 cups chicken stock
2   tablespoons drained green peppercorns in brine
1¹/2 teaspoons minced fresh thyme,
    or ¹/2 teaspoon dried thyme
2   teaspoons Dijon mustard
1/3 cup whipping cream
    Fresh thyme leaves

- Pat the pork medallions to flatten slightly. Season with salt and pepper.
- Melt 2 tablespoons of the butter in a heavy skillet over medium-high heat and add the medallions.
- Cook for 3 minutes per side or until brown. Remove to a platter using a slotted spoon, reserving the pan drippings.
- Melt the remaining 1 tablespoon butter with the reserved pan drippings and add the shallots. Sauté for 2 minutes.
- Stir in the vermouth and bring to a boil. Cook for 5 minutes or until reduced and of a glaze consistency.
- Stir in the stock, peppercorns and minced thyme. Boil for 10 minutes or until reduced to 1/4 cup. Whisk in the Dijon mustard and then the cream. Season with salt and pepper.
- Return the pork medallions and collected juices to the skillet and cook for 3 minutes or until the sauce thickens slightly.
- Divide evenly between dinner plates and sprinkle with fresh thyme leaves. Serve immediately.

Serves 4 to 6

Note: Serve with Celebration Cauliflower (page 171) and a green salad.

Roasted Pork Tenderloin with Cranberry Port Sauce

4¹/₂ teaspoons thyme
1¹/₂ teaspoons salt
1¹/₂ teaspoons freshly ground pepper
3   (1-pound) pork tenderloins, trimmed
3   tablespoons vegetable oil
    Cranberry Port Sauce (*page 125*)
1¹/₂ teaspoons grated orange zest

- Mix the thyme, salt and pepper in a small bowl.

- Pat the tenderloins dry with paper towels and brush with 2 tablespoons of the oil. Rub the surface of the tenderloins with the thyme mixture. The tenderloins may be covered and stored in the refrigerator at this point and roasted the next day.

- Heat the remaining 1 tablespoon oil in a heavy ovenproof skillet over high heat and add the tenderloins. Cook for 5 minutes or until brown on all sides.

- Roast the pork at 400 degrees for 20 minutes or until a meat thermometer inserted in the thickest part of the tenderloin registers 150 degrees for medium. Remove the tenderloins to a platter and cover to keep warm, reserving the pan drippings.

- Add the Cranberry Port Sauce and orange zest to the reserved pan drippings and bring to a simmer, stirring frequently.

- Cut the tenderloins into ¹/₂-inch slices and divide among eight plates. Drizzle some of the sauce mixture over the tenderloin and serve the remaining sauce on the side.

Serves 8

Note: *Serve with Pesto Rice Timbales (page 191) and Emerald Green Beans (page 168).*

Cranberry Port Sauce

3	tablespoons butter	2	cups fresh or frozen
2	cups chopped onions		cranberries (about 8 ounces)
4	garlic cloves, minced	1/2	cup sugar
1 1/2	teaspoons grated orange zest	1/4	cup tawny port
1 1/2	teaspoons dried sage leaves	1	tablespoon cornstarch
1	teaspoon dried thyme		Salt and freshly ground
2	cups chicken broth		pepper to taste
1 1/2	cups cranberry juice cocktail		

- Melt the butter in a large heavy skillet over high heat and add the onions. Sauté for 8 minutes or until golden brown.
- Add the garlic, orange zest, sage and thyme and cook for 1 minute, stirring constantly. Stir in the broth and cranberry juice cocktail and bring to a simmer.
- Simmer for 8 minutes or until the mixture is reduced to 2 1/2 cups, stirring frequently. Strain the sauce into a medium saucepan, pressing on the solids with the back of a spoon; discard the solids. Stir in the cranberries and sugar and bring to a boil.
- Boil for 5 minutes or until the cranberries pop. Stir in a mixture of the port and cornstarch and boil for 1 minute or until thickened.
- Season with salt and pepper. Store, covered, in the refrigerator.

Makes 4 cups

Note: *The tart flavor of this sauce goes well with pork, turkey or game. The sauce may be prepared up to one day in advance and stored, covered, in the refrigerator.*

Apricot-Stuffed Pork Loin

2 cups dry white wine
2 cups dried apricots
1/4 cup orange liqueur
1 (3¹/2-pound) center-cut pork loin, split into 2 portions
1 red onion, thinly sliced
1 tablespoon minced fresh basil
1 teaspoon minced fresh lemon thyme
1 teaspoon minced fresh marjoram
1 teaspoon minced fresh oregano
1/4 cup (1/2 stick) butter
1/4 cup vegetable oil
2 cups beef broth
1/4 cup cornstarch

- Combine the wine, apricots and liqueur in a bowl and marinate for 4 to 10 hours. Drain the apricots, reserving the liquid.

- Butterfly each pork portion, slashing across the grain to make even in thickness.

- Arrange the onion slices evenly over each portion and sprinkle evenly with the basil, lemon thyme, marjoram and oregano. Spoon the apricots down the center.

- Wrap both sides of each pork portion around the stuffing and tie at 1-inch intervals with kitchen twine, making sure that the apricots are secured.

- Heat the butter and oil in a heavy ovenproof skillet and add the pork. Cook until brown on all sides. Roast at 375 degrees until a meat thermometer registers 150 degrees for medium. Remove the pork to a platter, reserving the pan drippings.

- Whisk the broth and cornstarch in a bowl until blended. Whisk the cornstarch mixture and reserved apricot liquid into the reserved pan drippings.

- Heat until thickened, whisking constantly. Remove the kitchen twine from the pork and slice as desired. Serve with the sauce.

Serves 6

Note: A very elegant presentation. Make your butcher your best friend. Next time a recipe calls for butterflying a piece of meat, ask him to skin, trim, and butterfly it to save time in the kitchen.

Pork Loin with Red Currant Sauce

2	cups dried prunes	1	teaspoon freshly
1	cup red wine		ground pepper
1	cup port	1/4	cup all-purpose flour
2	tablespoons butter	1	cup beef broth
2	tablespoons olive oil	2	tablespoons red currant jelly
1	(3-pound) pork loin, cut into	1	cup heavy cream
	eight 1/2-inch-thick slices	1/4	cup finely chopped parsley
1	teaspoon salt		

- Soak the prunes in the red wine and port in a bowl for 12 hours. Pour the prune mixture into a saucepan. Simmer for 30 minutes or until the prunes are tender and the liquid is slightly reduced. Drain, reserving the liquid, and cover the prunes to keep warm.

- Heat the butter and olive oil in a skillet until the butter melts. Sear the pork on each side. Continue cooking for 3 minutes on each side.

- Remove the pork to a platter using a slotted spoon, reserving 2 tablespoons of the pan drippings. Sprinkle the pork with the salt and pepper. Cover to keep warm.

- Mix the flour with the reserved pan drippings until blended. Add the broth and reserved prune liquid and mix well. Stir in the jelly and cream and bring to a boil.

- Return the pork and prunes to the skillet and simmer over low heat for 15 minutes, stirring occasionally.

- Arrange the pork on a platter and drizzle with the sauce. Sprinkle with the parsley.

Serves 8

Carolina Baby Back Ribs

6   racks baby back ribs
    (about 9 pounds)
1/2 cup cider vinegar
4   teaspoons olive oil
1   cup minced onion
1 1/2 cups water
1   cup ketchup
2/3 cup packed light brown sugar
2/3 cup vinegar
1/4 cup molasses

2   tablespoons Worcestershire
    sauce
2   tablespoons (heaping) instant
    coffee granules
2   teaspoons Creole mustard
2   teaspoons chili powder
1   teaspoon ground cumin
1/4 teaspoon ground cinnamon
1/4 teaspoon cayenne pepper

- Brush both sides of the ribs with cider vinegar and chill for 2 hours.
- Heat the olive oil in a heavy large saucepan over medium heat and add the onion. Sauté for 5 minutes or until tender.
- Whisk in the water, ketchup, brown sugar, vinegar, molasses and Worcestershire sauce. Stir in the coffee granules, Creole mustard, chili powder, cumin, cinnamon and cayenne pepper. Bring to a boil. Reduce the heat. Simmer for 30 minutes or until reduced to 3 cups, stirring occasionally.
- Arrange the ribs meat side up in a single layer on two large baking sheets. Roast at 350 degrees for 1 3/4 hours. Cover loosely with foil if browning too quickly.
- Brush both sides of the ribs with 3/4 cup of the sauce and roast for 10 minutes. Brush both sides with additional sauce and roast for 15 minutes longer. Remove the ribs from the oven and let stand, covered with foil, for 15 minutes.
- Cut each of the racks into three- or four-rib sections and serve with the remaining sauce.

Serves 8

Note: The ribs can be cooked in a slow cooker with the sauce. The sauce may be stored in the refrigerator for up to one week.

Glazed Spiral Ham

6	garlic cloves	1/4	cup yellow mustard
1	cup packed brown sugar		Grated zest of 1 orange
1	(8-ounce) jar mango chutney	1/4	cup orange juice
1/4	cup Creole mustard	1	spiral-cut ham

- Pulse the garlic in a food processor until finely chopped. Add the brown sugar, chutney, Creole mustard, yellow mustard, orange zest and orange juice and process until blended.
- Pour the mustard mixture over the ham in a baking pan.
- Bake at 350 degrees for 1 hour or until heated through, basting frequently.

Variable servings

Note: The butcher can help you decide on the size of the ham required for the number of guests you are serving.

Sausage Campanelle

1	(19-ounce) package Italian sausage, casings removed	2	teaspoons Italian seasoning
1	onion, chopped	8	ounces cream cheese, cubed
2	garlic cloves, minced	4	quarts water
2	(14-ounce) cans diced tomatoes	2	tablespoons salt
		16	ounces campanelle pasta

- Cook the sausage, onion and garlic in a large skillet until the sausage is crumbly and the onion is translucent, stirring frequently; drain.
- Stir in the tomatoes and Italian seasoning and simmer for 5 minutes, stirring occasionally. Add the cream cheese and cook until the cream cheese melts, stirring frequently.
- Bring the water and salt to a boil in a stockpot and add the pasta. Cook until al dente and drain.
- Toss the warm pasta with the sausage mixture in a large bowl and serve immediately.

Serves 6

Barbecued Franks

1   cup ketchup
1/4   cup hot water
1/4   cup packed brown sugar
1/4   cup vinegar
3   tablespoons Worcestershire sauce
2   tablespoons all-purpose flour
2   teaspoons paprika
2   teaspoons chili powder or dry mustard
1/2   teaspoon salt
1/2   teaspoon freshly ground black pepper
1/8   teaspoon red pepper (optional)
2   onions, chopped
12   large frankfurters (about 3 pounds)
12   hot dog buns
      Coleslaw (optional) (*page 98*)

- Combine the ketchup, hot water, brown sugar, vinegar and Worcestershire sauce in a bowl.
- Mix the flour, paprika, chili powder, salt, black pepper and red pepper in a bowl and stir into the ketchup mixture. Add the onions and mix well.
- Arrange the frankfurters in a baking pan. Pour the ketchup mixture over the top.
- Bake at 350 degrees for 1 hour.
- Serve the frankfurters in buns topped with the Coleslaw.

Serves 12

Note: *Invite the neighborhood over to watch a football game. Ask them to bring a dish to complement the meal.*

Roasted Lemon Chicken

1 (2- to 3-pound) chicken	2 large lemons, thinly sliced
3 tablespoons fresh rosemary leaves, or 2 teaspoons dried rosemary	1 1/2 teaspoons salt
	1/4 teaspoon freshly ground pepper

■ Carefully loosen the skin from the chicken breast and drumsticks. Rub beneath the skin with the rosemary. Slip as many lemon slices under the skin as it takes to cover and pat the skin in place. Place any remaining lemon slices in the body cavity.

■ Sprinkle with the salt and pepper and place the chicken breast side up in a roasting pan.

■ Place in a preheated 450-degree oven. Reduce the heat to 350 degrees immediately. Roast for 20 minutes per pound or until cooked through, basting occasionally with the pan juices.

■ Serve with the pan juices. May substitute Cornish game hens for the chicken.

Serves 4

Note: *Serve with Caribbean Sweet Rice (page 190).*

Roasted Balsamic Chicken

1/4 cup balsamic vinegar	2 garlic cloves, crushed
2 tablespoons Dijon mustard	1 (2 1/2- to 3-pound) chicken, cut up
2 tablespoons lemon juice	1/2 cup chicken broth
2 tablespoons olive oil	1 teaspoon grated lemon zest
Salt and freshly ground pepper to taste	1 tablespoon parsley

■ Mix the vinegar, Dijon mustard, lemon juice, olive oil, salt, pepper and garlic in a bowl. Pour over the chicken in a shallow dish and turn to coat. Marinate, covered, in the refrigerator for 2 hours, turning occasionally.

■ Arrange the undrained chicken in a roasting pan. Roast at 350 degrees for 1 hour or until cooked through. Remove the chicken to a heated platter, reserving the pan drippings. Cover to keep warm.

■ Stir the broth, lemon zest and parsley into the reserved pan drippings and bring to a simmer. Drizzle over the chicken and serve immediately.

Serves 4

Grilled Chicken with Soy Vinaigrette

8   boneless skinless chicken breasts
1/4   cup olive oil
1/4   cup lemon juice
2   teaspoons dried thyme, or 1 tablespoon chopped fresh thyme
2   red bell peppers, cut into bite-size pieces
1   yellow bell pepper, cut into bite-size pieces
2   tablespoons (or more) olive oil
1   pound asparagus spears, trimmed and cut into bite-size pieces
  Soy Vinaigrette (*below*)

- Arrange the chicken in a single layer in a shallow dish.
- Whisk 1/4 cup olive oil, the lemon juice and thyme in a bowl and pour over the chicken, turning to coat. Marinate, covered, in the refrigerator for several hours, turning occasionally.
- Sauté the bell peppers in 2 tablespoons olive oil in a skillet until tender-crisp. Remove the bell peppers to a bowl using a slotted spoon, reserving the pan drippings.
- Sauté the asparagus in the reserved pan drippings until tender-crisp, adding additional olive oil if needed. Mix the asparagus with the bell peppers.
- Grill the chicken or sauté in a skillet until cooked through.
- Slice the chicken diagonally into thin slices and add to the bell pepper mixture. Add the Soy Vinaigrette and toss until coated.

Serves 8 to 10

Soy Vinaigrette

2   tablespoons sugar
2   tablespoons toasted sesame oil
2   tablespoons vegetable oil
2   tablespoons red wine vinegar
2   tablespoons soy sauce

- Whisk the sugar, sesame oil, vegetable oil, vinegar and soy sauce in a bowl until the sugar dissolves.

Makes 1/2 cup

Note: Serve with Lemon Rice (page 189). Use the vinaigrette as a marinade for meat, fish, or poultry. Marinate in a sealable plastic bag—no pan to wash.

Mustard Chicken

8   boneless skinless chicken breasts, trimmed
     Salt and freshly ground pepper to taste
3   green onions with tops, thinly sliced
2   or 3 garlic cloves, minced
2   to 3 tablespoons chopped fresh herbs (marigold mint, tarragon, thyme or dill weed)
3   tablespoons Dijon mustard
2   tablespoons butter, softened
1   tablespoon dry vermouth or white wine
2   teaspoons honey

- Place the chicken between sheets of plastic wrap or in a sealable plastic bag. Pound with a meat mallet or the back of a skillet until slightly flattened. Sprinkle the chicken with salt and pepper.

- Combine the green onions, garlic, fresh herbs, Dijon mustard, butter, vermouth and honey in a bowl, mixing to make a paste.

- Spoon about 1 1/2 teaspoons of the paste on each chicken breast and roll from the wider end to enclose the filling. Arrange seam side down in a lightly oiled baking dish and dot with the remaining paste.

- Bake at 350 degrees for 30 minutes or until the chicken is cooked through.

Serves 8

Chicken Florentine

All-purpose flour for coating
Salt and freshly ground pepper to taste
1 egg, lightly beaten
1 tablespoon water
1/2 cup dry bread crumbs
1/4 cup freshly grated Parmesan cheese
8 boneless skinless chicken breasts
1/2 cup (1 stick) butter
2 pounds fresh baby spinach
2 tablespoons butter
1 tablespoon lemon juice
1 pound baby bella mushrooms, sliced
2 tablespoons butter
Parsley

- Mix flour, salt and pepper in a shallow dish. Whisk the egg and water in a bowl until blended. Mix the bread crumbs and cheese in a shallow dish.

- Coat the chicken with the flour mixture, the egg mixture and the bread crumb mixture in the order listed. Arrange in a single layer on a baking sheet. Chill, covered, for 1 hour.

- Heat 1/2 cup butter in a skillet and add the chicken. Cook until brown on all sides. Reduce the heat and cook, covered, for 25 minutes or until the chicken is tender.

- Sauté the spinach in 2 tablespoons butter in a skillet until wilted. Stir in the lemon juice. Mound the spinach on a serving platter and top with the chicken. Cover to keep warm.

- Sauté the mushrooms in 2 tablespoons butter in the skillet until tender and spoon the mushrooms over the chicken. Garnish with parsley and serve immediately.

Serves 8

Goat Cheese-Stuffed Chicken Breasts with Sun-Dried Tomatoes

3 tablespoons chopped drained oil-pack sun-dried tomatoes
4 ounces mild goat cheese, crumbled
1/4 cup finely chopped shallots
3 tablespoons chopped fresh parsley
1 teaspoon minced garlic
1/2 teaspoon freshly ground pepper

8 boneless skinless chicken breasts
1 cup dry bread crumbs
Salt and freshly ground pepper to taste
1 egg white
1/4 teaspoon salt
1/4 cup (1/2 stick) butter
Sprigs of parsley

■ Reserve a small portion of the sun-dried tomatoes for garnish. Combine the remaining sun-dried tomatoes, goat cheese, shallots, chopped parsley, garlic and 1/2 teaspoon pepper in a bowl and mix well. (May process the mixture in a food processor until combined.)

■ Cut a pocket in the side of each chicken breast and fill the pockets evenly with the goat cheese mixture.

■ Mix the bread crumbs and salt and pepper to taste in a shallow dish. Whisk the egg white and 1/4 teaspoon salt in a bowl until combined.

■ Brush the chicken breasts with the egg white mixture and coat with the bread crumb mixture. Arrange the coated chicken on a plate and chill for 20 minutes.

■ Melt the butter in a skillet over medium-high heat and add the chicken, turning to coat evenly with the butter.

■ Reduce the heat to medium-low and cook, covered, for 3 minutes. Turn the chicken and cook, covered, until cooked through. Remove the chicken to a platter and garnish with parsley sprigs and the reserved sun-dried tomatoes.

Serves 8

Note: Use kitchen shears for cutting sun-dried tomatoes.

Chicken Supreme

4 (10-ounce) packages frozen chopped spinach, thawed and drained
6 boneless skinless chicken breasts
1/2 cup all-purpose flour
1/4 cup (1/2 stick) butter, melted
1/2 teaspoon garlic powder
2 cups whipping cream
1 cup (4 ounces) grated Parmesan cheese
Paprika

- Press the excess moisture from the spinach. Spread the spinach in a lightly greased 9×13-inch baking dish.
- Coat the chicken with the flour and dip in the butter.
- Arrange the chicken in a single layer over the spinach. Sprinkle with garlic powder and pour the cream over the top. Sprinkle with the cheese and dust with paprika.
- Bake at 325 degrees for 50 minutes.

Serves 6

Slow-Cooker Chicken Provençal

2 to 2 1/2 pounds boneless skinless chicken breasts or thighs
1 (14-ounce) can diced tomatoes
1 cup chicken broth
1 cup white wine
1 cup chopped onion
1 (6-ounce) jar marinated artichokes
1/2 cup pitted niçoise olives
1/2 cup drained pimento-stuffed green olives
1 tablespoon minced garlic
1 teaspoon herbes de Provence or Italian seasoning
Hot cooked rice or hot cooked pasta

- Combine the chicken, tomatoes, broth, wine, onion and undrained artichokes in a 3 1/2- to 4-quart slow cooker. Add the olives, garlic and herbs de Provence and mix well.
- Cook, covered, on Low for 7 to 8 hours, or on High for 3 1/2 to 4 hours or until the chicken is tender.
- Serve with rice or pasta.

Serves 6

Sunday Night Chicken

4	carrots
8	ounces fresh mushrooms
4	pounds chicken pieces
$1/2$	teaspoon salt
$1/4$	teaspoon freshly ground pepper
1	tablespoon (or more) butter
1	tablespoon (or more) vegetable oil
1	large leek, sliced (*see Note page 49*)
1	cup dry white wine
$1/2$	cup chicken stock
2	teaspoons minced fresh thyme

- Cut the carrots crosswise into halves and then lengthwise into halves, depending on the thickness. Slice the large mushrooms into halves.

- Sprinkle the chicken with the salt and pepper.

- Heat the butter and oil in a 12-inch sauté pan over medium-high heat until the foaming subsides and add the chicken. Sauté for 10 to 15 minutes or until brown on all sides, adding additional butter and oil if needed. Remove the chicken to a platter, reserving the pan drippings.

- Discard all but a thin coating of the butter mixture from the sauté pan. Add the carrots, mushrooms and leek. Sauté for 4 to 5 minutes or until the pan juices evaporate. Return the chicken and accumulated juices to the pan, moving the vegetables to the top.

- Add the wine, stock and thyme and bring to a boil. Reduce the heat to low and simmer, covered, for 25 minutes or until the chicken is cooked through, basting three or four times.

- Divide the chicken evenly among dinner plates and top with the vegetables. Ladle the pan juices over the chicken and vegetables. Serve immediately.

Serves 8

Thai Chicken Stir-Fry

1 (14-ounce) can coconut milk
1 cup water
1/2 teaspoon salt
1 cup long grain rice
3 tablespoons creamy peanut butter
1 tablespoon soy sauce
2 teaspoons chili garlic paste
1 tablespoon toasted sesame oil
2 boneless skinless chicken breasts, cut into bite-size pieces
1 red bell pepper, cut into thin strips
2 green onions, diagonally sliced

- Combine 1 cup of the coconut milk, the water and salt in a saucepan and bring to a boil. Stir in the rice and reduce the heat to low. Simmer, covered, for 20 minutes.

- Whisk the remaining coconut milk, peanut butter, soy sauce and chili garlic paste in a bowl until combined.

- Heat the sesame oil in a skillet over medium-high heat for 2 minutes. Add the chicken and stir-fry for 5 minutes or until brown. Add the bell pepper and green onions and cook, covered, for 10 minutes, stirring occasionally.

- Stir in the peanut butter mixture and bring to a boil. Cook for 3 minutes, stirring constantly.

- Serve the chicken mixture over the rice.

Serves 2 to 4

Note: *This recipe can easily be doubled. The dish takes on a smoky flavor when cooked in a wok. Chili garlic paste can be found in Asian markets or in the Asian section of most grocery stores.*

Chicken with Peking Sauce

2   teaspoons cornstarch
2   teaspoons soy sauce
2   teaspoons dry sherry
2   pounds boneless skinless
    chicken breasts,
    cut diagonally into
    bite-size pieces
9   tablespoons peanut oil

2   garlic cloves, minced
1   tablespoon minced fresh ginger
2   pounds snow peas, strings
    removed and julienned
1   cup water chestnuts, sliced
2/3 cup bamboo shoots, chopped
6   green onions with tops, sliced
    Peking Sauce (*below*)

- Mix the cornstarch, soy sauce and sherry in a large bowl and add the chicken. Add 3 tablespoons of the peanut oil and mix well. Marinate at room temperature for 15 minutes, stirring occasionally.

- Heat a wok or sauté pan over high heat and add 4 tablespoons of the remaining peanut oil. Add the garlic and ginger when the oil begins to heat and stir once. Stir in the chicken mixture and stir-fry for 4 minutes or until the chicken is cooked through. Remove the chicken mixture to a platter.

- Heat the remaining 2 tablespoons peanut oil in the wok and add the snow peas. Stir-fry for 1 minute. Stir in the water chestnuts, bamboo shoots and green onions.

- Stir-fry for 30 seconds and add the chicken mixture. Stir in the Peking Sauce and cook until thickened and bubbly.

Serves 10

Note: *Serve with Steamed Rice (page 189). The key to Asian cooking is to have all the ingredients ready before the cooking process begins.*

Peking Sauce

1/4 cup cornstarch
2   teaspoons sugar
1/2 teaspoon salt
1/2 cup chicken stock
1/4 cup hoisin sauce

2   tablespoons soy sauce
1   tablespoon chili purée
     (optional)
2   teaspoons red wine vinegar
1 1/2 teaspoons hot chili oil

- Mix the cornstarch, sugar and salt in a bowl.
- Stir in the stock, hoisin sauce, soy sauce, chili purée, vinegar and chili oil.

Makes about 1 cup

Indonesian Chicken-Fried Rice

3¹/₂ cups chicken broth
2   cups white rice
¹/₂ cup vegetable oil
2   cups chopped onions
3   garlic cloves, minced
2   cups julienned cooked chicken
1¹/₂ cups chopped cooked ham
1¹/₂ cups shrimp, peeled and deveined
¹/₄ cup peanut butter
2   tablespoons chopped unsalted cashews
1   teaspoon ground coriander
¹/₂ teaspoon ground cumin
¹/₂ teaspoon ground red pepper

- Combine the broth and rice in a saucepan and bring to a boil. Reduce the heat to low and cook, covered, for 20 minutes.

- Drain the rice and spread on a baking sheet. Let stand until cool.

- Heat the oil in a deep skillet and add the onions. Sauté for 10 minutes. Add the rice and garlic. Sauté for 1 minute.

- Add the chicken, ham, shrimp, peanut butter, cashews, coriander, cumin and red pepper. Cook over low heat for 10 minutes or until the shrimp barely turn pink, stirring occasionally.

Serves 6

Note: An exotic main dish needing no other embellishments. Serve with a cucumber salad and sliced fruit.

Curried Chicken and Artichoke Casserole

3 boneless skinless
  chicken breasts
1/2 teaspoon whole
  black peppercorns
1 onion, cut into quarters
1 or 2 bay leaves
1 tablespoon butter
1/2 cup chopped onion
2 garlic cloves, minced
8 ounces fresh button
  mushrooms, sliced
1 (14-ounce) can artichoke
  hearts, drained and
  cut into quarters
1 (10-ounce) can cream of
  chicken soup

2/3 cup chicken broth
1/2 cup mayonnaise
1 teaspoon curry power,
  or to taste
1 to 2 teaspoons fresh
  lemon juice
  Salt and freshly ground
  pepper to taste
4 ounces Cheddar cheese,
  shredded
  Seasoned bread crumbs
  Melted butter

- Poach the chicken, peppercorns, onion and bay leaves in water in a skillet. Remove from the heat and cool the chicken in the poaching liquid.

- Melt 1 tablespoon butter in a skillet and add the onion and garlic. Sauté until the onion is translucent. Add the mushrooms. Cook until the liquid evaporates and remove from the heat.

- Drain the chicken and pat dry. Slice the chicken and add to the mushroom mixture. Stir in the artichokes gently.

- Mix the soup, broth, mayonnaise, curry powder, lemon juice, salt and pepper in a bowl. Add to the chicken mixture with the cheese and mix well.

- Spoon the chicken mixture into a baking dish and sprinkle with a mixture of bread crumbs and melted butter. Bake at 350 degrees for 30 to 45 minutes or until brown and bubbly.

Serves 4 to 6

Note: *Poach the chicken in white wine, if desired.*

Crowd-Pleasing Turkey Tetrazzini

32 ounces spaghetti
3 cups chopped celery
2 cups chopped green bell pepper
1 cup sliced fresh mushrooms
1/2 cup chopped onion
1 1/2 cups (3 sticks) butter
1/2 cup all-purpose flour
4 cups milk
1 cup white wine
1 pound extra-sharp Cheddar cheese, shredded
6 cups chopped cooked turkey
1/4 cup Worcestershire sauce
1/4 cup lemon juice
4 teaspoons salt
1/2 teaspoon freshly ground pepper

- Cook the spaghetti using the package directions. Drain and keep warm.
- Cook the celery, bell pepper, mushrooms and onion in the butter in a large skillet until the onion is translucent.
- Add the flour and stir until combined. Add the milk and wine gradually, stirring constantly.
- Cook until thickened, stirring constantly. Add the cheese, turkey, Worcestershire sauce, lemon juice, salt and pepper. Cook until the cheese melts, stirring constantly.
- Spoon the sauce over the hot spaghetti on a serving platter.

Serves 10 to 12

Note: *The sauce may be frozen for future use.*

Sweet Spiced Duck Breasts

8	ounces butternut squash, chopped	1¹/₂	teaspoons cardamom, toasted and finely ground
4	garlic cloves	1¹/₂	teaspoons coriander, toasted and finely ground
3	tablespoons chopped fresh thyme	1¹/₂	teaspoons star anise, toasted and finely ground
4	shallots, cut into halves	1¹/₂	teaspoons peppercorns, toasted and finely ground
	Dash of ground cinnamon or Chinese five-spice powder		
3	tablespoons olive oil	4	boneless duck breasts
8	ounces assorted fresh mushrooms, coarsely chopped		Salt and freshly ground pepper to taste
1	tablespoon sherry vinegar or balsamic vinegar	3	tablespoons butter
		3	ounces dried cranberries, chopped
1	teaspoon garlic salt		
	Freshly ground pepper to taste		Walnut oil (optional)

- Combine the squash, garlic, thyme, shallots and cinnamon or Chinese five-spice powder in a roasting pan and drizzle with the olive oil, tossing to coat.

- Roast at 350 degrees for 30 to 45 minutes. Add the mushrooms, vinegar, garlic salt and pepper and mix well. Roast for 20 minutes longer.

- Combine the cardamom, coriander, star anise and peppercorns in a small bowl and mix well. Rub the cardamom mixture over the outer surface of the duck breasts and season with salt and pepper.

- Sear the ducks breast side up in a sauté pan over medium heat. Turn and cook until the desired degree of doneness. Remove to a platter to rest and drain the pan drippings.

- Heat the butter in the same sauté pan and cook until light brown. Add the squash mixture and cranberries and cook just until heated through, stirring occasionally.

- Brush the duck breasts with walnut oil and slice diagonally.

- Serve with the roasted vegetables.

Serves 4

Note: *Serve with Goat Cheese and Chive Potato Cakes (page 180).*

Hoisin-Roasted Cornish Game Hens

2   tablespoons minced fresh ginger
2   fresh red chiles, seeded and minced
3   garlic cloves, minced
4   Cornish game hens
1   bunch fresh cilantro, trimmed
1/2 cup hoisin sauce

- Mix the ginger, red chiles and garlic in a bowl. Rub the ginger mixture over the outer surface of the game hens. Fill the inside cavities with the cilantro and truss.

- Chill, covered, for 20 minutes.

- Brush the game hens with the hoisin sauce and arrange in a single layer in a baking pan.

- Roast at 375 degrees for 30 minutes. Discard the trussing string and serve.

Serves 4

Chutney-Glazed Cornish Game Hens

6   Cornish game hens
     Apricot Almond Stuffing (*page 187*), unbaked and cooled
     Salt and freshly ground pepper to taste
1/4 cup (1/2 stick) butter, melted and cooled
1/3 cup fresh lemon juice
1   (8-ounce) jar mango chutney

- Pat the game hens dry with paper towels. Chill, uncovered, for several hours.

- Loosely stuff the cavities with the unbaked Apricot Almond Stuffing and truss. Sprinkle with salt and pepper. Arrange the game hens on a foil-lined rack in a roasting pan; do not allow to touch. Brush with the butter. Roast at 400 degrees in the upper third of the oven for 1 hour.

- Combine the lemon juice, chutney, salt and pepper in small saucepan and bring to a boil, stirring constantly. Remove from the heat and cool slightly.

- Purée in a blender or food processor to make a glaze. Brush the game hens with the glaze and roast for 15 minutes longer or until golden brown.

- Discard the trussing string and arrange on a platter. Serve immediately.

Serves 6

Flotilla Party

In the fall, avid boaters begin designing their intricate themes for the upcoming annual Thanksgiving holiday flotilla, a boat parade. Family traditions have been built around holiday flotillas, so join in the festivities. The biggest debate is whether it's more fun to participate in the parade or watch it from a boat or your deck. It's a moveable feast!

"What's This" Spread
Capered Deviled Eggs
Sesame Beef Strips
Chicken and Spinach Salad with Pearl Couscous
Crunchy Pea Salad
Tortellini Salad with Sun-Dried Tomatoes

Orange Chocolate Chip Cookies
Crispy Oatmeal Cookies
Chocolate Layer Bars

Spiced Iced Tea

Elliot Daingerfield (American, 1859–1932)
Lotus Land, c.1920
Oil on canvas
Purchased with funds from the Jessie N. Howell Memorial North Carolina Acquisitions Fund,
Takeda Chemical and Tabitha McEachern

Seafood

The Cook's Canvas 2

Italian Baked Oysters

2²/3 cups seasoned bread crumbs
1 cup grated Parmesan cheese
2 teaspoons salt
2 teaspoons oregano
1 teaspoon freshly ground
   black pepper
1/2 teaspoon basil

1/4 teaspoon cayenne pepper
1 cup chopped green onions
1/2 cup chopped parsley
1/4 cup chopped garlic
1¹/4 (2¹/2 sticks) cups butter
1 cup olive oil
4 quarts oysters, drained

- Combine the bread crumbs, cheese, salt, oregano, black pepper, basil and cayenne pepper in a bowl and mix well.
- Sauté the green onions, parsley and garlic in the butter and olive oil in a large skillet until tender. Stir in the bread crumb mixture. Remove from the heat. Fold in the oysters and spoon into two 9×12-inch baking dishes. Bake at 350 degrees for 15 minutes or until brown and crisp.

Serves 12

Picante Fried Oysters

1 pint select oysters, drained
1 cup buttermilk
1/2 cup all-purpose flour
1/4 cup yellow cornmeal
2 teaspoons paprika
1 teaspoon chili powder
1 teaspoon red pepper

1 teaspoon garlic powder
1 teaspoon dried oregano
1/4 teaspoon dry mustard
1 teaspoon salt
1/2 teaspoon freshly ground
   black pepper
Vegetable oil for frying

- Combine the oysters and buttermilk in a sealable plastic bag and marinate in the refrigerator for 2 hours or longer.
- Combine the flour, cornmeal, paprika, chili powder, red pepper, garlic powder, oregano, dry mustard, salt and black pepper in a bowl and mix well.
- Drain the oysters, discarding the buttermilk. Dredge the oysters in the flour mixture.
- Fry the oysters in 370-degree vegetable oil in a skillet until brown; drain. Serve with Low-Country Tartar Sauce (*page 209*) or Pecan Tartar Sauce (*page 208*).

Serves 4

Pan-Seared Scallops

3   tablespoons extra-virgin
    olive oil
12 large sea scallops
1/4 cup dry white wine

2   tablespoons butter
    Juice of 1 lemon
1/4 cup minced parsley

■ Heat a cast-iron skillet until hot enough for a drop of water to sizzle in the skillet.

■ Pour the olive oil into the hot skillet and swirl the skillet to spread the oil.

■ Add the scallops and cook for 4 minutes. Turn the scallops over and add the wine gradually. Cook for 2 minutes and add the butter, shaking the skillet to distribute the butter.

■ Add the lemon juice and the parsley and cook for 1 minute. Remove to a warm plate to serve.

Serves 4

Seafood Newburg

1   pound bay scallops
8   cups water
    Seafood seasoning
1   pound small shrimp,
    peeled and deveined
1   cup (2 sticks) butter
1/2 cup all-purpose flour
5   cups milk

4   ounces Cheddar cheese,
    shredded
1   pound lobster meat or lump
    crab meat (*see Note page 22*)
2   tablespoons butter
1/4 cup sherry
    Pinch of salt
    Paprika and parsley

■ Cook the scallops in a saucepan of boiling water seasoned with seafood seasoning for 2 to 3 minutes or until opaque and slightly firm. Remove the scallops, reserving the boiling liquid in the saucepan. Add the shrimp and simmer for 2 to 3 minutes or until the shrimp turn pink. Drain, discarding the liquid.

■ Melt 1 cup butter in a skillet and stir in the flour until smooth to make a roux. Cook for 5 minutes, stirring constantly. Do not brown. Scald the milk in a small saucepan. Add the milk to the roux gradually, stirring constantly, until thick. Stir in the cheese.

■ Sauté the lobster meat, scallops and shrimp in 2 tablespoons butter in a skillet until hot. Add the seafood mixture, sherry and salt to the sauce and stir gently until mixed. Spoon into a large serving bowl. Garnish with paprika and parsley.

Serves 6

Frogmoor Stew Party

10 bay leaves
1/2 (6-ounce) container Old Bay
   seafood seasoning
3 cans beer
1/2 (5-ounce) bottle hot red
   pepper sauce
12 links hot sausage, cut into
   1-inch pieces

12 small ears frozen sweet corn,
   thawed
18 small new potatoes, cooked
3 pounds heads off shrimp,
   unpeeled
   Coleslaw (*page 98*)
   Pimento Corn Sticks
   (*page 73*)

■ Combine the bay leaves and Old Bay seasoning in a large stockpot with enough
   water to fill 2/3 full. Bring to a boil. Add the beer, hot sauce and sausage and boil
   for 8 minutes. Stir.

■ Add the corn and boil using the package directions. Add the potatoes to the
   stockpot and boil until heated through. Add the shrimp and boil for 90 seconds
   or until the shrimp turn pink. Drain and spread the sausage, shrimp and vegetables
   across a newspaper-lined table. Serve with the Coleslaw and Pimento Corn Sticks.

Serves 6

Masonboro Sound Shrimp

1 cup each chopped red and
   yellow bell pepper
1/2 cup small red onion or
   Vidalia onion, chopped
2 tablespoons butter, melted
1 cup cream
1 tablespoon chopped fresh
   dill weed
1 tablespoon Worcestershire
   sauce

1 teaspoon apple cider vinegar
1 teaspoon salt
1/2 teaspoon dry mustard
1/4 teaspoon red pepper
1 pound cooked shrimp,
   peeled and deveined
1 cup fresh bread crumbs
3 tablespoons drained and
   rinsed capers

■ Sauté the bell peppers and onion in the butter in a saucepan until tender. Add the
   next 7 ingredients. Cook until thickened, stirring frequently.

■ Remove from the heat and fold in the shrimp, bread crumbs and capers. Spoon into
   a 2-quart baking dish. Bake at 375 degrees for 10 minutes or until heated through.

Serves 6

Shrimp and Feta Linguini

6	ounces linguini	1/2	cup chopped onion
1/2	cup ricotta cheese	12	ounces shrimp, peeled
1/4	cup chopped parsley		and deveined
1	egg, lightly beaten	1	small tomato, peeled
	Salt and pepper to taste		and chopped
2	garlic cloves, minced	1	tablespoon water
1/4	cup fresh basil, chopped	2	teaspoons cornstarch
1	tablespoon olive oil	1/2	cup tomato sauce
1	tablespoon butter	2	ounces mozzarella
1 1/2	cups sliced mushrooms		cheese, shredded
1/2	cup chopped green	1/2	cup crumbled feta cheese
	bell pepper		

- Cook the pasta in boiling salted water until al dente; drain.
- Combine the ricotta cheese, parsley and egg in a small bowl and mix well. Season with salt and pepper. Add the pasta and toss until coated.
- Press the pasta mixture over the bottom and up the side of a greased 9-inch round baking dish, making a crust.
- Sauté the garlic and basil in the olive oil and butter in a skillet for 30 seconds, stirring constantly.
- Add the mushrooms, bell pepper, onion and shrimp. Sauté for 4 minutes or until the shrimp turn pink and the vegetables are tender. Stir in the tomato.
- Combine the water and cornstarch in a small bowl and mix until dissolved. Stir into the shrimp mixture and cook until thickened, stirring constantly.
- Spoon the shrimp mixture into the pasta-lined baking dish and spread the tomato sauce on the top. Cover the pasta crust with foil. Bake at 350 degrees for 20 minutes.
- Sprinkle with the mozzarella cheese and feta cheese. Bake, uncovered, for 5 minutes longer or until the cheese melts.

Serves 4

Note: *This recipe may be doubled and baked in a large ovenproof pasta serving dish.*

Baked Shrimp with Linguini

3/4 cup (1 1/2 sticks) butter
1/4 cup olive oil
2 tablespoons minced garlic
2 tablespoons lemon juice
1 tablespoon chopped
   fresh parsley
1 teaspoon Worcestershire
   sauce
1 teaspoon fresh oregano, or
   1/2 teaspoon dried oregano
1 teaspoon fresh basil
1 teaspoon fresh tarragon

1/2 teaspoon dry mustard
1/2 teaspoon crushed red pepper
1/4 teaspoon salt
2 pounds shrimp, peeled
   and deveined
1/2 cup wine
1 pound linguini
16 cups water
1 to 2 tablespoons salt
1 cup (4 ounces) freshly grated
   Parmesan cheese

- Heat the butter and olive oil in a saucepan until the butter is melted. Add the garlic, lemon juice, parsley, Worcestershire sauce, oregano, basil, tarragon, dry mustard, crushed red pepper and 1/4 teaspoon salt. Simmer until the garlic is translucent and remove from the heat.

- Dip the shrimp in the sauce to coat and place on a foil-lined baking dish.

- Add the wine to the remaining sauce and bring to a boil. Reduce the heat and simmer until the sauce is reduced by one-fourth. Spoon the sauce over the shrimp.

- Cook the pasta in the boiling water with 1 to 2 tablespoons salt in a stockpot until al dente; drain.

- Bake the shrimp at 400 degrees for 7 minutes or until pink.

- Combine the pasta, shrimp and sauce in a large serving bowl, tossing to mix. Serve with the Parmesan cheese on the side.

Serves 6

Note: This is a wonderful way to cook shrimp. Roasting seafood in an oven sears the outside and keeps the inside moist and flavorful.

Four "Side Boy" Shrimp

4	garlic cloves, finely chopped
1	tablespoon peanut oil
1	pound shrimp, peeled and deveined
1	cup canned or fresh chopped pineapple
1	tablespoon fish sauce
1	tablespoon brown sugar
2	tablespoons curry powder
1/4	teaspoon red pepper flakes
3	green onions, thinly sliced
4	cups hot cooked rice
1/2	cup chopped peanuts
1/3	cup chopped parsley or cilantro
1/3	cup chopped red bell pepper
1/3	cup toasted shredded coconut

- Sauté the garlic in the peanut oil in a wok until tender.

- Add the shrimp and sauté until the shrimp turn pink. Remove the garlic and shrimp from the pan with a slotted spoon and set aside, reserving the pan drippings in the wok.

- Add the pineapple, fish sauce, brown sugar, curry powder and red pepper flakes to the pan drippings and sauté for 2 to 3 minutes.

- Return the garlic and shrimp to the wok. Add the green onions and sauté for 1 minute.

- Divide the rice among four soup or pasta bowls. Spoon the shrimp mixture on top. Serve the peanuts, parsley, bell pepper and coconut in separate small decorative bowls. Let your guests top their dish with the "side boy" accompaniments of their choice.

Serves 4

Note: In India, accompaniments are referred to as "boys," which usually number about ten. You may also use chutney or sliced bananas.

Shrimp Cakes with Watercress Rémoulade

1/2 cup minced sweet onion	2 pounds cooked shrimp, peeled, deveined and coarsely chopped
1/3 cup butter	
1/2 cup all-purpose flour	
2 cups milk, warmed	1 cup panko bread crumbs
1 tablespoon seafood seasoning	1/2 cup vegetable oil
1/2 teaspoon cayenne pepper	Watercress Rémoulade (*below*)
2 eggs, lightly beaten	

- Sauté the onion in the butter in a skillet over medium heat for 3 minutes or until translucent. Whisk in the flour and cook for 1 minute, whisking constantly.
- Add the milk gradually, whisking constantly until combined. Cook until thickened, stirring constantly with a wooden spoon.
- Remove from the heat and stir in the seafood seasoning and cayenne pepper. Let stand until cool.
- Whisk in the eggs. Fold in the shrimp and panko bread crumbs.
- Shape into sixteen cakes and place on a baking sheet. Chill, covered, for 2 hours.
- Cook the cakes in the oil in a large deep skillet over medium-high heat for 4 to 5 minutes on each side or until golden brown. Drain on paper towels. Serve with the Watercress Rémoulade.

Serves 8

Watercress Rémoulade

1 1/2 cups mayonnaise	3 green onions, sliced
1 1/2 cups chopped watercress leaves	2 tablespoons Dijon mustard
1/2 cup chopped fresh chives	1 garlic clove, minced
	1/4 teaspoon red pepper

- Combine the mayonnaise, watercress, chives, green onions, Dijon mustard, garlic and red pepper in a bowl and mix well. Store in the refrigerator.

Makes 2 cups

Note: *This sauce may be served with fish or boiled shrimp as an appetizer.*

Crab and Shrimp Casserole

1	cup wild rice	1	cup mayonnaise
1	pound shrimp	1	cup chopped celery
	Salt to taste	3/4	cup half-and-half
8	ounces mushrooms, sliced	1/2	red bell pepper, chopped
3	tablespoons butter	1/2	cup chopped onion
2	(13-ounce) cans artichoke hearts, drained and chopped	1	tablespoon Worcestershire sauce
1	pound crab meat (see Note page 22)		Freshly ground pepper to taste

- Cook the rice according to the package directions.
- Cook the shrimp in boiling salted water in a saucepan until the shrimp turn pink; drain. Peel and devein the shrimp.
- Sauté the mushrooms in the butter in a saucepan for 5 minutes or until tender.
- Remove from the heat and add the shrimp, artichoke hearts, crab meat, mayonnaise, celery, half-and-half, bell pepper, onion and Worcestershire sauce; mix well. Season with salt and pepper. Spoon into a large baking dish.
- Bake at 375 degrees for 30 minutes or until heated through and bubbly.

Serves 8

Carolina Deviled Crab

2 1/4	cups fresh bread crumbs	1	teaspoon grated onion
1/2	cup milk		Dash of hot red pepper sauce
1	cup mayonnaise	1	pound lump crab meat
4	hard-cooked eggs, mashed		(see Note page 22)
2	teaspoons Worcestershire sauce		Toasted bread crumbs

- Combine the fresh bread crumbs and milk in a mixing bowl and mix well.
- Add the mayonnaise, eggs, Worcestershire sauce, onion and hot sauce and mix well. Fold in the crab meat. Spoon into ten crab shell molds or ramekins. Sprinkle with toasted bread crumbs.
- Bake at 350 degrees for 15 minutes or until brown and bubbly.

Serves 5

Crab Cakes with Shrimp Sauce

1	small red bell pepper, chopped	1	tablespoon minced fresh parsley
1	small onion, chopped		
1	large rib celery, chopped	1	tablespoon hot red pepper sauce
1	tablespoon olive oil		
1	(6-ounce) package panko bread crumbs		Salt and freshly ground pepper to taste
3/4	cup mayonnaise	1	pound crab meat
1	egg, lightly beaten		(*see Note page 22*)
1	tablespoon seafood seasoning	2	tablespoons vegetable oil
			Shrimp Sauce (*below*)

■ Sauté the bell pepper, onion and celery in the olive oil in a skillet until tender. Drain and let stand until cool.

■ Combine the sautéed vegetables, 1 cup of the panko, the mayonnaise, egg, seafood seasoning, parsley, hot sauce, salt and pepper in a bowl; mix well. Fold in the crab meat. Shape the crab meat mixture into cakes 2 1/2 inches in diameter and 3/4 inch thick. Coat the crab cakes on both sides with the remaining panko. Chill until firm.

■ Sauté in the vegetable oil in a skillet for 4 minutes on each side. Serve hot with the Shrimp Sauce spooned over the top. To bake the crab cakes, place on a greased baking sheet and bake at 350 degrees for 10 minutes. Increase the oven temperature to 450 degrees and bake for 10 minutes longer or until brown.

Serves 8

Shrimp Sauce

2 1/2	tablespoons butter	2	tablespoons whole grain mustard
3 1/2	tablespoons all-purpose flour		
2	cups hot milk	1/2	teaspoon salt
1	pound cooked shrimp, peeled and deveined		Pinch of white pepper
			Hot red pepper sauce

■ Melt the butter in a heavy saucepan. Add the flour and stir to make a roux. Cook over medium heat for 2 minutes, stirring constantly. Add the hot milk gradually and cook until thickened, whisking constantly. Stir in the shrimp, whole grain mustard, salt, white pepper and hot sauce and cook for 3 minutes, stirring frequently.

Makes about 4 cups

Spicy Catfish with Vegetables and Basil Cream Sauce

1   (16-ounce) package frozen whole kernel corn, thawed
1   onion, chopped
1   green bell pepper, chopped
1   red bell pepper, chopped
2   tablespoons butter
3/4 teaspoon salt
3/4 teaspoon freshly ground pepper
1   teaspoon garlic powder
1/2 cup all-purpose flour

1   tablespoon Creole seasoning, or to taste
4   (6- to 8-ounce) catfish fillets
1/3 cup buttermilk
1   tablespoon butter
1   tablespoon vegetable oil
1/2 cup whipping cream
2   tablespoons chopped fresh basil
Sprigs of basil

- Sauté the corn, onion and bell peppers in 2 tablespoons butter in a skillet for 6 to 8 minutes or until tender.

- Stir in the salt, pepper and garlic powder. Spoon the corn mixture into a serving dish and keep warm.

- Combine the flour and Creole seasoning in a large shallow dish and mix well.

- Dip the catfish in the buttermilk, coating well, and dredge in the seasoned flour, shaking off any excess.

- Heat 1 tablespoon butter and the oil in a skillet over medium-high heat. Cook the catfish in batches in the hot butter mixture for 2 to 3 minutes on each side or until golden brown. Add additional butter and oil if necessary.

- Arrange the catfish on top of the corn mixture.

- Add the cream and basil to the pan drippings in the skillet. Cook, scraping the bottom of the pan to loosen the brown bits from the bottom of the skillet. Simmer for 1 to 2 minutes or until thickened, stirring frequently.

- Serve the sauce on the side. Garnish with basil sprigs.

Serves 4

Note: You may substitute flounder or grouper for the catfish.

Glorious Grouper with Dill Sauce

3   pounds fresh grouper fillets
     Sea salt to taste
     Lemon pepper to taste
1   large onion, chopped
1   cup sliced mushrooms
1/2   cup chopped chives
1   tablespoon vegetable oil
1   cup dry white wine

2   tablespoons butter, melted
2   tablespoons lemon juice
3   lemons, thinly sliced
1   tablespoon finely chopped
     fresh dill weed
1   tablespoon chopped parsley
     Dill Sauce (*below*)

- Season the grouper with sea salt and lemon pepper.
- Arrange the onion, mushrooms and chives in the bottom of a baking dish brushed with the oil. Season with salt and lemon pepper.
- Arrange the grouper on top of the vegetables and pour the wine over the fish.
- Combine the butter and lemon juice in a small bowl and mix well. Brush over the grouper. Arrange the lemon slices on top and sprinkle with the dill weed and parsley.
- Bake at 350 degrees for 20 to 25 minutes or until cooked through.
- Serve with the Dill Sauce on the side.

Serves 6 to 8

Dill Sauce

1   egg
1 1/2 cups sour cream
2   tablespoons finely chopped
     fresh dill weed
4   teaspoons lemon juice

2   teaspoons grated onion
1   teaspoon sugar
1   teaspoon salt
1/8   teaspoon curry powder
     Pinch of white pepper

- Whisk the egg in a bowl until smooth. Add the sour cream, dill weed, lemon juice, onion, sugar, salt, curry powder and white pepper and whisk until combined. Chill, covered, until serving time.

Makes 2 cups

Note: *If you are concerned about using raw eggs, use eggs pasteurized in their shells, which are sold at some specialty food stores, or use an equivalent amount of pasteurized egg substitute.*

Swordfish Steaks with Caribbean Salsa

1/2 cup soy sauce
1/2 cup vegetable oil
1 green bell pepper, sliced
1 garlic clove, minced
2 tablespoons lemon juice
2 tablespoons lime juice

2 teaspoons Dijon mustard
1 teaspoon grated lemon zest
6 swordfish steaks
Caribbean Salsa (*below*)
Finely chopped parsley

- Combine the soy sauce, vegetable oil, bell pepper, garlic, lemon juice, lime juice, Dijon mustard and lemon zest in a bowl and mix well.
- Add the swordfish, coating well with the marinade. Marinate, covered, in the refrigerator for 2 hours.
- Remove the swordfish with a slotted spoon, reserving the marinade.
- Place the swordfish on a grill rack and grill for 5 to 6 minutes on each side or to the desired degree of doneness, brushing often with the reserved marinade.
- Spoon the Caribbean Salsa onto six dinner plates and top with the grilled swordfish. Garnish with parsley.

Serves 6

Caribbean Salsa

2 mangos, chopped
1 pineapple, chopped
1 bunch green onions, chopped
1 green bell pepper, chopped
1 red bell pepper, chopped

1 jalapeño chile, chopped (optional)
1/2 cup chopped fresh cilantro
3 tablespoons vegetable oil

- Combine the mangos, pineapple, green onions, bell peppers, jalapeño chile, cilantro and oil in a bowl and mix well.
- Chill, covered, in the refrigerator until serving time.

Makes 8 cups

Note: This salsa can be served with grilled fish, pork or chicken.

Seared Ahi Tuna with Caponata Relish

4 (6-ounce) Ahi tuna steaks
   Kosher salt and freshly
   ground pepper to taste
1/4 cup olive oil

Caponata Relish (*below*)
Freshly grated Parmesan
cheese
Chopped chives

- Season the tuna with salt and pepper.
- Sear the tuna in the olive oil in a heavy skillet over medium-high heat for 3 to 4 minutes per side or to the desired degree of doneness.
- Place the tuna on four dinner plates and spoon the Caponata Relish on top. Sprinkle with Parmesan cheese and chives. Serve immediately.

Serves 4

Caponata Relish

1/4 cup red wine vinegar
1/4 cup sugar
1/2 cup chopped onion
1/3 cup olive oil
1 1/2 tablespoons minced garlic
1 large eggplant, peeled and
   finely chopped

3/4 teaspoon salt
2 cups seeded and chopped
   tomatoes (about 4 large)
1 cup pine nuts, toasted
3/4 cup chopped green olives
1/3 cup chopped fresh
   basil leaves

- Heat the vinegar and sugar in a small saucepan over medium heat until dissolved, stirring occasionally. Remove from the heat and let stand until cool.
- Sauté the onion in the olive oil in a skillet over medium-high heat for 3 minutes.
- Add the garlic and sauté for 30 seconds. Add the eggplant and salt and sauté for 5 minutes or until tender. Add the tomatoes and cook for 10 to 12 minutes or until the liquid evaporates and the mixture thickens, stirring frequently.
- Stir in the pine nuts and olives. Add enough vinegar mixture 1 tablespoon at a time until the desired flavor and consistency are reached, mixing well after each addition.
- Remove from the heat and stir in the basil. Adjust the seasonings to taste.

Makes 4 cups

Note: *This relish may also be served as an appetizer with Toasted Pita Chips (page 69).*

Roasted Salmon with Mustard Dill Sauce

4   (6-ounce) salmon fillets (skin on)
     Salt and freshly ground pepper to taste
1   teaspoon olive oil
2   teaspoons butter
     Mustard Dill Sauce (*below*)

- Season the salmon with salt and pepper.
- Heat the olive oil in an ovenproof skillet over high heat. Add the salmon skin side down.
- Add the butter and shake the skillet, blending the butter with the olive oil as it melts. Cook for 4 minutes.
- Bake at 450 degrees for 5 minutes or until the salmon is cooked through.
- Serve with the Mustard Dill Sauce.

Serves 4

Note: *Serve with Capered Mashed Potatoes (page 182).*

Mustard Dill Sauce

1   cup Dijon mustard
1   cup fresh dill weed
1/2 cup mayonnaise
1/2 cup sugar
1/3 cup white wine vinegar
2   tablespoons vegetable oil

- Combine the mustard, dill weed, mayonnaise, sugar and vinegar in food processor or blender. Process until smooth.
- Add the oil gradually, processing constantly until blended. Store, chilled, in the refrigerator.

Makes 3 cups

Baked Salmon with Artichoke Hearts

1   (1 to 1 1/2-pound) salmon fillet
1   (12-ounce) can artichoke
    hearts, cut into halves
1/4   cup lemon juice

1/4   cup (1/2 stick) butter, melted
1   (5-ounce) container Boursin
    cheese spread
    Fresh chopped basil

- Slice the salmon lengthwise into 1/2-inch-wide strips and place in a buttered baking dish. Place artichoke hearts between each strip. Drizzle with the lemon juice.
- Blend the butter and cheese spread in a bowl. Pour evenly over the salmon and sprinkle with basil. Bake at 350 degrees for 20 minutes.

Serves 4

Pistachio-Crusted Salmon with Wilted Greens

2 1/2   pounds salmon, cut into
      6 fillets
3/4   cup pistachios
1 1/2   cups mayonnaise
1 1/2   teaspoons horseradish
1 1/2   teaspoons ground pepper

1 1/2   teaspoons lemon juice
1/4   teaspoon salt
2   pounds baby bok choy,
    sliced, or 1 1/2 pounds baby
    spinach leaves
    Olive oil

- Place the salmon skin side down on a baking sheet.
- Pulse the pistachios in a food processor with a sharp blade until coarsely ground. Do not overprocess. Combine the pistachios, mayonnaise, horseradish, pepper, lemon juice and salt in a bowl and mix well. Spread on top of the salmon.
- Bake at 425 degrees for 20 minutes. Remove the salmon from the baking sheet with a spatula, letting the skin stick to the baking sheet. (For easier cleanup, place baking sheet immediately in hot water to loosen the skin.)
- Sauté the bok choy or baby spinach in batches in hot olive oil in a skillet until each batch is wilted before adding the next. Divide among six dinner plates, topping each with a salmon fillet.

Serves 6

Note: You may serve this dish with Braised Baby Bok Choy (page 166) instead. Pair this dish with Lemon Rice (page 189) or a mixture of brown rices.

Elegant Dinner Party

Carolina moonrise over the Atlantic calls for an elegant dinner party. There is nothing like the warm weather and the smell of jasmine. Open the doors, have your guests dress in their finest, and celebrate life.

Shrimp Endive

Ginger Dip with crackers and vegetables

Spiced-Up Nuts

Pistachio-Crusted Salmon with Wilted Greens

Lemon Rice

Grand Marnier Carrot Bundles

Watercress and Orange Salad with Orange Vinaigrette

Roquefort Popovers

Chocolate Amaretti Torte

Unknown (American, mid-nineteenth century)
Detail of slave-made quilt, Tulip design, c. 1850
Cotton pieced quilt with double row stitching
Gift of Mildred and James Guthrie

Vegetables & Side Dishes

The Cook's Canvas 2

Sesame Asparagus

2 pounds pencil-thin asparagus
Juice of 1 lemon
1 tablespoon toasted sesame oil
1 tablespoon oyster sauce

2 teaspoons sesame seeds
Freshly ground pepper
to taste

- Snap off the woody ends of the asparagus spears.
- Arrange the asparagus lying in the same direction in a 3-quart rectangular baking dish.
- Whisk the lemon juice, sesame oil and oyster sauce in a bowl until blended. Stir in the sesame seeds and pepper.
- Pour the marinade over the asparagus and gently toss until completely coated. Microwave, tightly covered with plastic wrap, on High for 3 to 6 minutes or until tender. Serve hot.

Serves 6

Note: You may prepare this dish in advance, marinating the asparagus, covered, in the refrigerator for up to 24 hours. Microwave as directed.

Braised Baby Bok Choy

4 heads baby bok choy, sliced
into halves lengthwise
2 tablespoons olive oil

1 teaspoon salt
1/2 teaspoon pepper

- Cook the bok choy in the olive oil in a skillet over medium-high heat until seared on one side.
- Turn the bok choy over and turn off the heat. Cover and let stand for 5 minutes or until cooked through. Season with the salt and pepper.

Serves 4

Glazed Broccoli with Almonds

2 pounds fresh broccoli, separated into spears	4 ounces Cheddar cheese, shredded
1/2 teaspoon salt	2 tablespoons sherry
3/4 cup chicken broth	2 tablespoons lemon juice
1 cup half-and-half	Dash of freshly ground pepper
1/4 cup (1/2 stick) butter	1/4 cup slivered almonds
1/4 cup all-purpose flour	

- Cook the broccoli in enough salted water to cover in a saucepan until tender-crisp; drain. Arrange in a 9×12-inch baking dish.
- Heat the broth in a small saucepan and stir in the half-and-half. Remove from the heat. Melt the butter in a saucepan. Add the flour and stir to make a roux. Add the warm broth mixture and cook until thick, stirring constantly.
- Add the cheese and stir until melted. Stir in the sherry, lemon juice and pepper.
- Pour the sauce evenly over the broccoli and sprinkle with the almonds.
- Bake at 375 degrees for 30 minutes. Serve hot.

Serves 6 to 8

Steamed Savoy Cabbage with Bacon

12 ounces sliced bacon, cut into 1/2-inch pieces	3 tablespoons butter
1 large head Savoy cabbage (about 2 pounds)	3 tablespoons extra-virgin olive oil
6 large garlic cloves, minced	Salt and freshly ground pepper to taste

- Sauté the bacon in a skillet until crisp and brown. Drain on paper towels, reserving the bacon drippings in the skillet.
- Cut the cabbage into halves. Core the cabbage and slice lengthwise.
- Steam the cabbage for 10 minutes or until tender-crisp. Set the cabbage aside, covered, in a large serving bowl and keep warm.
- Heat the garlic, butter and olive oil in saucepan until the butter is melted.
- Drizzle the warm garlic butter over the cabbage and toss until coated. Season with salt and pepper and sprinkle with the bacon.

Serves 8

Orange Balsamic Cabbage

1 (2- to 2 1/2-pound) head cabbage, cored and coarsely chopped
1 large onion, coarsely chopped (about 1 cup)
2 tablespoons water
1/2 cup orange marmalade
3 tablespoons balsamic vinegar
3 tablespoons butter, melted
Grated zest of 1 orange

- Place the cabbage and onion in a microwave-safe glass baking dish and sprinkle with the water. Microwave, tightly covered, on High for 10 to 12 minutes or until tender-crisp, stirring once.
- Remove the cabbage with a slotted spoon and arrange on a serving plate.
- Combine the marmalade, vinegar and butter in a bowl and mix well.
- Drizzle the cabbage with some of the sauce and serve the remaining sauce on the side. Sprinkle with the orange zest.

Serves 12

Emerald Green Beans

2 pounds green beans, trimmed
Salt to taste
2 1/2 teaspoons grated fresh ginger
3/4 cup walnuts, chopped
1/2 cup golden raisins
1/4 cup (1/2 stick) butter
1/4 cup fresh lemon juice
Freshly ground pepper to taste

- Cook the green beans in enough boiling salted water to cover in a saucepan for 5 minutes or until tender-crisp; drain. Submerge the green beans in an ice water bath immediately until cool; drain.
- Sauté the ginger, walnuts and raisins in the butter in a skillet over medium-high heat for 2 to 3 minutes.
- Add the green beans and lemon juice. Lower the heat and cook until the beans are heated through, stirring frequently. Season with salt and pepper.

Serves 6 to 8

Note: This dish is a fresh and colorful accompaniment to any entrée and is one of our favorite recipes.

Green Bean Tivoli

1	pound young green beans
1/3	cup extra-virgin olive oil
1/4	cup minced green onions
2	tablespoons Dijon mustard
2	tablespoons lemon juice
1	tablespoon apple cider vinegar
1	tablespoon fresh or dried dill weed
2	teaspoons sugar
	Salt to taste
1/4	teaspoon pepper
1/3	cup sliced grape tomatoes
1/3	cup chopped pecans or walnuts, toasted

- Snap the ends off the green beans. Cook in enough water to cover in a large saucepan for 5 to 7 minutes or just until tender; drain. Rinse under cold running water until the beans are cool. Drain again and place in a bowl.

- Whisk the olive oil, green onions, Dijon mustard, lemon juice, vinegar, dill weed, sugar, salt and pepper in a bowl until blended. Pour over the green beans. Toss until well coated.

- Chill, covered, for 2 hours or longer. Fold in the tomatoes and pecans just before serving.

Serves 4 to 6

Note: *When serving this dish in a glass bowl, stand medium-size tomato slices up around the side of the bowl. Fill in with the green bean mixture.*

Grand Marnier Carrot Bundles

4	large carrots		Dash of allspice
3	tablespoons butter		Dash of cinnamon
3	tablespoons light brown sugar		Dash of nutmeg
3	tablespoons Grand Marnier	10	to 12 chives

- Cut the carrots into 1/2×3-inch sticks.
- Steam until tender-crisp; drain.
- Combine the butter, brown sugar, Grand Marnier, allspice, cinnamon and nutmeg in a saucepan and cook until the mixture is smooth, stirring frequently.
- Add the carrots and cook over low heat, tossing until the carrots are well glazed.
- Divide the carrots into eight bundles and tie tightly with the chives. Place in a microwave-safe serving dish.
- Microwave on High for 1 minute or until heated through just before serving.

Serves 8

Carrot Soufflé

2	pounds carrots, cooked and mashed	2	teaspoons baking powder
		2	teaspoons vanilla extract
6	eggs, lightly beaten		Cinnamon to taste (optional)
1	cup granulated sugar		Freshly grated nutmeg to
1	cup packed light brown sugar		taste (optional)
6	tablespoons all-purpose flour		

- Combine the carrots, eggs, granulated sugar, brown sugar, flour, baking powder, vanilla, cinnamon and nutmeg in a food processor. Process until puréed.
- Pour the carrot mixture into a soufflé dish or baking dish.
- Bake at 350 degrees for 1 hour or until the soufflé comes away from the side of the dish and the top is light brown.

Serves 6 to 8

Stir-Fried Carrots, Kale and Walnuts

12	ounces kale	2	carrots, peeled and julienned
1/2	cup walnut pieces	1/4	teaspoon red pepper flakes
1	teaspoon vegetable oil	3/4	teaspoon freshly ground
3	slices fresh ginger		black pepper
2	large garlic cloves, finely	2	to 4 tablespoons vegetable
	chopped		broth
2	teaspoons vegetable oil		Soy sauce to taste

- Tear the leaves of the kale from the stalks, discarding the stalks. Roll the leaves and cut into 1/8-inch strips. Cut the strips into halves.

- Stir-fry the walnuts in 1 teaspoon oil in a large heated wok for 1 minute or until toasted. Drain on paper towels and set aside. Stir-fry the ginger and garlic in 2 teaspoons oil in the wok for 10 seconds or until fragrant.

- Add the carrots, red pepper flakes and black pepper. Stir-fry for 1 minute. Add the kale and toss until coated. Press the kale down and cover. Cook for 30 seconds.

- Stir in 2 tablespoons of the vegetable broth. Cook, covered, for 3 minutes, stirring every minute and adding additional vegetable broth as needed for steam.

- Remove and discard the ginger slices. Season with soy sauce and sprinkle with the walnuts. Serve hot.

Serves 3 to 4

Note: *Pair this dish with steamed fish and rice.*

Celebration Cauliflower

2	heads cauliflower, separated	1/2	cup cream
	into florets	1/4	cup (1/2 stick) butter
2	leeks, sliced (white part only)		Salt and freshly ground
2	cups chicken broth		pepper to taste

- Simmer the cauliflower, leeks and broth in a saucepan until tender; drain. Cook on low heat until dry. Do not brown.

- Purée the cauliflower mixture in a food processor with a steel blade in two batches until smooth. Add the cream and butter and pulse until blended. Spoon into a serving bowl. Season with salt and pepper.

Serves 8

Carolina Collard Greens with Cornmeal Dumplings

1	bunch collard greens (about 1³/4 pounds)	1	red bell pepper, chopped
1	pound mustard greens		White wine
6	slices thick-cut bacon		Red pepper flakes to taste
1	large onion, chopped		Cornmeal Dumplings (*below*)

- Rinse the collard greens and mustard greens three or four times in water or until no longer gritty; drain. Remove and discard tough stems. Chop the leaves.
- Cook the bacon in a stockpot until crisp.
- Layer the greens, onion and bell pepper one-half at a time in the stockpot. Add enough equal parts white wine and water to cover. Season with red pepper flakes.
- Cook, covered, over medium heat for 3 hours or until tender.
- Place the Cornmeal Dumplings on top of the greens and simmer for 3 to 4 minutes.
- Spoon several leaves and some of the juices over the dumplings. Cook for 15 minutes or until the dumplings are cooked through.

Note: Add three or four whole pecans to the saucepan to keep the smell of cooking greens from filling your house.

Cornmeal Dumplings

¹/4	cup shortening	¹/2	teaspoon baking powder
2	cups cornmeal	1	teaspoon salt
¹/2	cup all-purpose flour		Water

- Combine the shortening, cornmeal, flour, baking powder and salt in a bowl and mix well.
- Add water gradually just until the dry ingredients come together to make a dough, stirring constantly.
- Shape by ¹/4 cupfuls into balls and flatten to ¹/2 to 1 inch thick.

Serves 6

Caramelized Corn

1/2 cup sliced shallots
1/2 cup (1 stick) butter
2 (14-ounce) cans corn, or
  2 (16-ounce) packages frozen
  extra-sweet corn, thawed

Thyme to taste
Salt and white pepper to taste
Juice of 2 limes

- Sauté the shallots in the butter in a skillet until light brown.
- Add the corn and cook for 5 minutes or until golden brown, stirring frequently. Season with thyme, salt and white pepper. Let stand until room temperature. Stir in the lime juice just before serving.

Serve 6

Note: This dish may be cooked 3 to 4 hours in advance. When boiling fresh corn in water, add a pinch of sugar to the water to help bring out the corn's sweetness.

Eggplant à la Chilindron

1 red onion, chopped
6 garlic cloves, finely chopped
3 tablespoons extra-virgin
  olive oil
2 (2 1/2-pound) eggplants,
  cut into cubes
2 red or yellow bell peppers,
  cut into 1-inch pieces
15 pitted green olives

15 pitted black Greek olives
1 1/2 cups dry sherry
1 cup tomato sauce or
  tomato purée
1/2 cup chopped cilantro
1/8 teaspoon sugar
  Fresh thyme to taste, or
  1/2 teaspoon dried thyme
  Hot red pepper sauce to taste

- Sauté the onion and garlic in 2 tablespoons of the olive oil in a saucepan over medium-high heat until light golden brown. Do not overbrown.
- Add the remaining 1 tablespoon olive oil and the eggplant and sauté until light brown. Add the bell peppers and increase the heat. Sauté until the bell peppers are tender.
- Stir in the olives, sherry, tomato sauce or tomato purée, cilantro, sugar, thyme and hot sauce. Simmer, covered, over low heat for 35 to 40 minutes.

Serves 4

Stuffed Portobellos

4	portobello mushrooms, stems removed
	Olive oil for cooking
	Salt and freshly ground pepper to taste
2	cups baby spinach leaves
4	pieces roasted red bell pepper, chopped (*see Note page 19*)
4	slices buffalo mozzarella cheese or goat cheese

- Sauté the mushrooms in olive oil in a skillet for several minutes on each side or just until cooked through. Let stand until cool. Place the mushrooms bottom side up on a baking sheet. Season with salt and pepper.
- Sauté the spinach in olive oil in the skillet until wilted. Spoon the spinach onto each mushroom.
- Top each mushroom with a piece of roasted bell pepper and a slice of cheese.
- Bake at 350 degrees for 10 to 15 minutes or until heated through. Serve immediately.

Serves 4

Variation: You may substitute chopped roasted eggplant or chopped tomato for the roasted bell pepper. Or, stuff the portobellos with chopped fresh tomatoes and Niçoise olives sautéed in olive oil with herbes de Provence and chopped basil. Top with feta cheese and bake as directed.

Baked Mushrooms

1	tablespoon minced garlic
1/4	cup (1/2 stick) butter
1	pound mushrooms, sliced
1/4	cup sherry (optional)
8	ounces heavy cream
4	ounces mozzarella cheese, shredded
	Dash of cayenne pepper

- Sauté the garlic in the butter in a skillet over medium heat until tender.
- Add the mushrooms and sauté until the liquid evaporates. Add the sherry and cook until the sherry evaporates. Add the cream and cook until thickened, stirring constantly.
- Spoon the mixture into a baking dish and sprinkle evenly with the cheese and cayenne pepper.
- Bake at 350 degrees for 20 minutes or until heated through and the cheese is melted.

Serves 4

Mushroom Ring

2	tablespoons chopped onion	1/4	teaspoon freshly
1/4	cup (1/2 stick) butter		ground pepper
1	pound mushrooms, chopped	1	cup milk
1/4	cup all-purpose flour	4	eggs, lightly beaten
1/2	teaspoon salt		Creamed Sweet Peas (below)
1/4	teaspoon nutmeg		or cooked herb-seasoned rice
			Sprigs of parsley

- Sauté the onion in the butter in a saucepan over low heat until golden brown. Add the mushrooms and sauté for 5 minutes. Stir in the flour, salt, nutmeg and pepper. Add the milk and cook until thickened, stirring constantly. Remove from the heat and stir in the eggs.

- Pour the mixture into a buttered ring mold. Bake at 350 degrees for 30 minutes or until firm. Unmold onto a serving platter. Fill the center with Creamed Sweet Peas or herb-seasoned rice, if desired. Garnish with parsley.

Serves 6

Creamed Sweet Peas

1	cup sliced mushrooms	1	(16-ounce) package frozen
2	tablespoons butter		sweet peas, thawed
2	slices bacon, chopped		and drained
1	tablespoon chopped onion		Salt and freshly ground
1	tablespoon all-purpose four		pepper to taste
1	cup half-and-half, heated		

- Sauté the mushrooms in the butter in a small skillet for 1 minute; set aside.

- Cook the bacon in a large saucepan over low heat until it begins to brown. Add the onion and sauté until translucent.

- Stir in the flour to make a roux. Cook until the mixture bubbles, stirring constantly. Add the half-and-half gradually, stirring constantly until thickened. Stir in the mushrooms and peas. Season with salt and pepper.

Serves 6

Note: *Serve as a side dish or spoon into the center of the Mushroom Ring (above).*

Okra Fritters

1/4 cup cornmeal	2 tablespoons freshly grated
1/4 cup all-purpose flour	Parmesan cheese
1/2 cup chopped onion	1/4 teaspoon cayenne pepper
1/2 cup evaporated milk	2 cups sliced okra
1 egg, lightly beaten	(about 2/3 pound)
3 tablespoons chopped	Vegetable oil or peanut oil
fresh parsley	for frying
1/2 teaspoon salt	Salt to taste

- Combine the cornmeal and flour in a bowl and mix well. Add the onion, evaporated milk, egg, parsley, salt, cheese and cayenne pepper and mix well. Stir in the okra.
- Drop by tablespoonfuls into 350-degree oil in a deep heavy skillet. Fry until golden brown, turning once; drain on paper towels. Season with salt. Serve immediately.

Serves 8

Variation: These may also be served as an appetizer. For green tomato fritters, substitute 2 cups chopped green tomatoes for the okra and 1/2 cup goat cheese for the Parmesan cheese. Add additional cornmeal if the batter is too thin.

Three-Onion Casserole

2 large yellow onions, sliced	2 (5-ounce) containers Boursin
1 1/2 cups (6 ounces) shredded	garlic and herb cheese spread
Havarti cheese	4 leeks, thinly sliced
1 tablespoon butter	(*see Note page 49*)
Salt and freshly ground	6 ounces Gruyère cheese,
pepper to taste	shredded
2 large red onions, thinly sliced	2 tablespoons butter
	1/2 cup dry white wine

- Layer the yellow onions and Havarti cheese in a 3-quart baking dish greased with 1 tablespoon butter. Season with salt and pepper. Continue layering with the red onions, Boursin cheese, leeks and Gruyère cheese. Season with salt and pepper.
- Dot with 2 tablespoons butter and pour the wine evenly over the top. Bake at 350 degrees for 1 hour. Cover with foil to prevent overbrowning if necessary.

Serves 6

Baby Onions with Spinach and Parmesan Cheese

2   pounds baby onions
1   garlic clove, minced
2   tablespoons butter
1   pound spinach, stems
    removed
1/2 cup freshly grated
    Parmesan cheese

1/4 cup heavy cream
    Salt and freshly ground
    pepper to taste
1/4 cup freshly grated
    Parmesan cheese
2   tablespoons dry bread crumbs
1   tablespoon butter

- Place the onions in enough water to cover in a saucepan. Bring to a boil. Reduce the heat and simmer for 7 to 10 minutes or until tender-crisp; drain.

- Let stand until cool enough to handle. Remove the skins and trim the root ends.

- Sauté the garlic in 2 tablespoons butter in a saucepan over medium heat for 1 to 2 minutes or until fragrant.

- Add the spinach and cook for 5 minutes or until wilted and the liquid evaporates, stirring frequently; remove from the heat and stir in 1/2 cup cheese and the cream.

- Add the onions. Season with salt and pepper; mix well. Spoon the onion mixture into a 1-quart baking dish.

- Combine 1/4 cup cheese and the bread crumbs in a small bowl and mix well.

- Sprinkle evenly over the onions and dot with 1 tablespoon butter.

- Bake at 400 degrees for 20 minutes or until brown.

Serves 8

Note: You may use three (10-ounce) packages frozen pearl onions instead of the fresh. This will save time because the frozen onions do not have to be peeled and trimmed after cooking.

Onion, Raisin and Garlic Compote

1	pound pearl onions	2	tablespoons sugar
24	to 30 garlic cloves	1/2	teaspoon salt
1	bay leaf	1/2	cup raisins
1/4	cup (1/2 stick) butter	1	tablespoon fresh thyme, or
1 1/2	cups tawny port		to taste
1/4	cup white wine vinegar		Salt and pepper to taste

- Place the onions in enough water to cover in a saucepan. Bring to a boil and cook for 2 minutes. Drain and rinse under cold water until cool. Peel and trim the root ends.
- Sauté the garlic and bay leaf in butter in a saucepan over medium-low heat for 6 minutes or until the garlic is golden brown.
- Add the port, vinegar, sugar and salt. Simmer for 8 minutes. Add the onions and raisins and simmer for 9 minutes or until the onions are tender, stirring occasionally.
- Remove from the heat and stir in the thyme. Discard the bay leaf. Season with salt and pepper. Serve warm.

Makes 2 cups

Roasted Potatoes with Caramelized Garlic

2	tablespoons olive oil	1/4	cup balsamic vinegar
6	red potatoes, cut into 1-inch pieces	2	tablespoons white wine
		1/3	cup chopped fresh basil
16	garlic cloves, thinly sliced		Freshly ground pepper
2	tablespoons olive oil	1	tablespoon chopped
1	tablespoon sugar		fresh parsley

- Heat 2 tablespoons olive oil on a baking sheet at 425 degrees for 5 minutes. Add the potatoes and toss until coated. Bake for 30 to 35 minutes or until tender.
- Cook the garlic, covered, in 2 tablespoons olive oil in a skillet over very low heat for 5 to 8 minutes or until tender. Uncover and sprinkle with the sugar. Sauté until the garlic is golden brown. Add the vinegar, wine and basil and simmer for 2 minutes.
- Spoon the potatoes into a serving bowl and drizzle with the garlic mixture. Season with pepper and sprinkle with the parsley.

Serves 4 to 6

Garlic-Crusted Baked Potatoes

2   heads garlic
1¹/₂ tablespoons vegetable oil
1   teaspoon salt
¹/₄ teaspoon freshly ground pepper
6   Yukon Gold potatoes or red potatoes
¹/₄ cup vegetable oil
     Salt and pepper to taste
1   bunch fresh thyme

- Bake the garlic, wrapped in foil, at 425 degrees for 1 hour or until tender and golden brown. Let stand until cool enough to handle.

- Cut the tops of the garlic bulbs off just low enough to expose the cloves. Squeeze the garlic from the root end to the top into a bowl.

- Add 1¹/₂ tablespoons oil, 1 teaspoon salt and ¹/₄ teaspoon pepper and mix to make a paste.

- Cut the potatoes horizontally into 1-inch-thick slices. Spread a generous amount of the garlic mixture between each slice. Reassemble the potatoes, pressing well so that the slices stick together.

- Place each potato on a piece of foil. Drizzle each with 2 teaspoons oil and season with salt and pepper. Wrap tightly in the foil. Place on a baking sheet.

- Bake at 475 degrees for 1 hour and 10 minutes or until the potatoes are tender and the bottoms are encrusted with the caramelized garlic mixture. Arrange on a bed of thyme sprigs on a serving plate.

Serves 6

Goat Cheese and Chive Potato Cakes

1   pound Russet potatoes,
       peeled and cut into
       1-inch pieces
6   large shallots, sliced
2   garlic cloves, sliced
1/2 cup dry bread crumbs
31/2 ounces mild goat
       cheese, softened

1/4 cup minced fresh chives
1   tablespoon minced fresh sage
       Salt and freshly ground
       pepper to taste
1/2 cup dry bread crumbs
1/4 cup (1/2 stick) butter

- Place the potatoes, shallots and garlic in enough water to cover by 1 inch in a saucepan. Simmer for 10 to 15 minutes or until the potatoes are tender. Drain and cook over low heat until the mixture is dry.

- Press through a potato ricer or put through a food mill with a medium disc into a large bowl.

- Stir in 1/2 cup bread crumbs, the goat cheese, chives and sage. Season with salt and pepper.

- Shape the mixture into 3/4-inch-thick patties. Coat the patties on both sides with 1/2 cup bread crumbs.

- Sauté in the hot butter for 5 minutes on each side or until golden brown.

Serves 4

Note: Pair this dish with Beef Tenderloin (page 116) or a pork tenderloin. For an elegant luncheon dish, top each potato cake with a slice of ham, a poached egg and hollandaise sauce.

Potato, Leek and Turnip au Gratin

1   large garlic clove
1   tablespoon butter, softened
8   ounces potatoes, peeled and cut into $1/4$-inch-thick slices
8   ounces turnips, peeled and cut into $1/4$-inch-thick slices
2   leek bulbs, cut into rings (*see Note page 49*)
     Salt and freshly ground pepper to taste
     Freshly ground nutmeg to taste
2   cups heavy cream
1   large garlic clove, minced
$1/3$ cup shredded Gruyère cheese
$1/4$ cup freshly grated Parmesan cheese
2   tablespoons butter

- Cut 1 garlic clove into halves. Rub the bottom and sides of a gratin dish or baking dish with the cut sides of the garlic; discard garlic. Grease the dish with softened butter.
- Place the potatoes, turnips and leeks flat onto paper towels and pat the tops with paper towels to absorb the moisture. Season with salt, pepper and nutmeg.
- Arrange potato and turnip slices alternately in rows in prepared gratin dish. Sprinkle leeks between slices.
- Combine the cream and minced garlic clove together. Pour the cream evenly over the top and gently shake the baking dish, filling the spaces with the cream.
- Sprinkle with the Gruyère and Parmesan cheeses. Dot the top with 2 tablespoons butter. Bake at 450 degrees for 45 to 60 minutes or until the potatoes are tender. Cover with foil to prevent overbrowning if necessary.

Serves 6

Note: For the best flavor, peel the turnips past the faint dark line inside the peel.

Capered Mashed Potatoes

4 large Idaho potatoes, peeled and cut into quarters	1/2 cup coarsely chopped scallions
Salt to taste	1/2 cup drained capers
1 1/4 cups heavy cream	2 tablespoons chopped fresh dill weed
1/4 cup (1/2 stick) butter	Freshly ground pepper to taste
3/4 cup coarsely chopped onion	

- Place the potatoes in enough salted water to cover in a large saucepan. Bring to a boil. Cook for 15 minutes or until tender. Drain and cook over low heat, gently shaking the saucepan until the potatoes are dry.
- Simmer the cream and butter in a small saucepan over low heat for 15 minutes or until reduced to 1 cup. Mash the potatoes with a potato masher. Add the cream mixture, onion, scallions, capers and dill weed. Season with salt and pepper.

Serves 4

Note: This dish can stand at room temperature for up to 1 hour. Reheat gently, stirring often or keep warm in a slow cooker. Pair this dish with Roasted Salmon with Mustard Dill Sauce (page 161).

Potato Casserole

6 white potatoes	2 cups sour cream
1/2 cup (1 stick) butter	1 cup (4 ounces) shredded Cheddar cheese
1 (10-ounce) can cream of chicken soup	1/2 cup green onions, chopped

- Place the potatoes in enough water to cover in a saucepan and bring to a boil. Cook just until tender; drain. Process the potatoes in a food processor until chopped or mash with a potato masher in a large bowl.
- Heat the butter in the saucepan and stir in the soup. Add the butter mixture, sour cream, cheese and green onions to the potatoes and mix well. Spoon into a 2 1/2-quart buttered baking dish. Bake at 350 degrees for 45 minutes. Let stand for 15 minutes before serving.

Serves 6

Note: You may sprinkle this dish with French-fried onions before baking.

Praline Sweet Potatoes

3 cups cooked sweet potatoes
2 eggs, lightly beaten
1/2 cup milk
1/4 cup butter (1/2 stick), melted
1 teaspoon vanilla extract
1/2 teaspoon salt
1 (10-ounce) package chopped pecans
1 cup packed light brown sugar
1/2 cup self-rising flour
1/4 cup (1/2 stick) butter, melted

- Combine the sweet potatoes, eggs, milk, 1/4 cup melted butter, the vanilla and salt in a mixing bowl and mix well with an electric mixer. Spoon into a buttered baking dish.
- Combine the pecans, brown sugar, flour and 1/4 cup melted butter in a bowl and mix well. Sprinkle evenly on top of the sweet potato mixture.
- Bake at 350 degrees for 30 to 45 minutes or until set.

Serves 6

Note: *Sweet potatoes may be baked, boiled, or cooked in the microwave. Peel and measure. This is a natural holiday dish but may be enjoyed all year long.*

Tomatoes Stuffed with Summer Squash

1	pound yellow squash, shredded	1	large garlic clove, minced
1	pound zucchini, shredded	2	tablespoons olive oil
2	teaspoons salt	2	tablespoons butter
8	small tomatoes	1	cup heavy cream
	Olive oil for brushing	4	ounces Gruyère cheese, shredded
	Salt and pepper to taste	1/2	cup freshly grated Parmesan cheese
1	onion, minced		

- Toss the squash and zucchini with 2 teaspoons salt and let stand in a colander for 30 minutes. Squeeze out the moisture in a tea towel.

- Cut 3/4 inch off the tops of the tomatoes and discard. Scoop out the insides of the tomatoes with a demitasse spoon, discarding the seeds and juices. Do not squeeze the tomatoes.

- Place the tomatoes cut side down on a baking sheet. Brush with olive oil and sprinkle with salt and pepper.

- Bake at 325 degrees for 10 minutes. Invert the tomatoes on a wire rack over a baking sheet and let stand for 30 minutes or until drained.

- Sauté the onion and garlic in 2 tablespoons olive oil and 2 tablespoons butter in a skillet over medium-high heat until translucent.

- Add the squash and zucchini and sauté for 2 minutes.

- Add the cream and season with salt and pepper. Cook until the cream has been absorbed, stirring frequently. Remove from the heat.

- Stir in the Gruyère cheese and 1/4 cup of the Parmesan cheese.

- Spoon the squash mixture into the tomatoes, mounding on top.

- Place the tomatoes on a rack in a broiler pan and sprinkle with the remaining 1/4 cup Parmesan cheese. Broil 5 inches from the heat source for 3 to 4 minutes or until bubbly and golden brown. Arrange on a heated serving platter.

Serves 8

Vegetable Gratin

1	onion, thinly sliced	1	cup heavy cream
2	tablespoons olive oil	2	eggs
1	eggplant, chopped	1/4	cup shredded Parmesan cheese
8	ounces zucchini, sliced	3	tablespoons balsamic vinegar
8	ounces yellow squash, sliced	1	tablespoon olive oil
2	garlic cloves, finely chopped		Freshly ground pepper to taste
	Salt to taste	2	tablespoons Parmesan cheese

■ Cook the onion in 2 tablespoons olive oil in a skillet for 15 to 20 minutes or until tender and golden brown, stirring occasionally. Add the eggplant and sauté for 3 to 4 minutes. Add the zucchini, squash and garlic and sauté until tender. Season with salt. Remove from the heat and let stand until cool.

■ Beat the cream, eggs, 1/4 cup Parmesan cheese, the vinegar and 1 tablespoon olive oil in a bowl until combined. Season with salt and pepper. Add the vegetable mixture and mix well. Spoon into a 9-inch baking dish.

■ Bake, covered with foil, at 325 degrees for 35 to 40 minutes. Uncover and sprinkle with 2 tablespoons Parmesan cheese. Broil until the top is golden brown.

Serves 4

Note: Pair this dish with an arugula, tomato and basil salad.

Baked Vegetable Medley

2	Japanese eggplants	1/2	cup freshly grated Parmesan
1	small sweet onion		cheese, crumbled feta cheese
2	plum tomatoes		or chèvre
2	zucchini or yellow squash	1/4	cup olive oil or flavored oil
2	red or yellow bell peppers		(*see page 108*)
			Chopped fresh basil leaves
			Salt and freshly ground pepper

■ Slice the eggplant, onion, tomatoes, zucchini or yellow squash and bell peppers in a food processor with a slicing attachment.

■ Arrange the vegetables in an oiled baking dish. Sprinkle with the cheese, olive oil, basil, salt and pepper. Bake, covered with foil, at 375 degrees for 15 minutes. Uncover and bake until the vegetables are tender.

Serves 8

Roasted Vegetables

2¹/₂ pounds mixed vegetables of choice, such as

    asparagus
    beets, quartered
    green bell peppers, cut into 1-inch pieces
    red bell peppers, cut into 1-inch pieces
    brussels sprouts, cut into halves if large
    butternut squash, cut into 1¹/₂-inch cubes
    carrots, cut into thirds, or baby carrots
    garlic cloves
    mushrooms
    onions, quartered
    potatoes, sliced into ¹/₂-inch rounds
    yellow squash, sliced into ¹/₂-inch rounds
    zucchini, sliced into ¹/₂-inch rounds

3   tablespoons olive oil or flavored oil (*see page 108*)
    Chopped fresh herbs of choice (*see Note*)
    Kosher salt and freshly ground pepper to taste

■ Combine the vegetables, olive oil, herbs, salt and pepper on a baking sheet. Toss until well coated. Spread in a single layer.

■ Bake at 425 degrees for 20 minutes for smaller vegetables to 40 minutes for larger vegetables or until the vegetables are tender on the inside and crisp on the outside.

Serves 6

Note: Use fresh herbs such as thyme, rosemary, tarragon or basil.

The Right Stuffing

5	pounds red potatoes, peeled and cut in half	1	cup (2 sticks) butter, softened
1	pound mild Italian sausage, casings removed	2	teaspoons chopped sage
1	pound bulk pork sausage	1	teaspoon salt
		1/4	teaspoon freshly ground pepper

- Place the potatoes in enough cold water to cover in a saucepan. Bring to a boil and simmer until the potatoes are just tender; drain. Chop into smaller pieces.

- Cook all the sausage in a skillet until just pink, stirring until crumbly; drain on paper towels. Combine with the potatoes in a large bowl.

- Add the butter, sage, salt and pepper and mix well. Spoon into a 3-quart greased baking dish. Bake at 350 degrees for 30 minutes or until heated through.

Serves 12

Note: For color, leave the potato skins on and add chopped parsley. This recipe will stuff a 22-pound turkey. Allow stuffing to cool before stuffing the turkey.

Apricot Almond Stuffing

1	large Spanish onion, minced		Salt and freshly ground pepper to taste
1	shallot, minced		
1	garlic clove, minced	1/2	cup white wine
6	tablespoons butter	4	cups white bread cubes
1/2	cup dried apricots, chopped	3/4	cup almonds, skinned, chopped and lightly toasted
1/3	cup golden raisins		
3/4	teaspoon dried sage	1/4	cup chicken stock
1/8	teaspoon ground cloves		

- Cook the onion, shallot and garlic in the butter in a saucepan over low heat until golden brown, stirring occasionally. Add the apricots, raisins and seasonings.

- Cook for 1 minute, stirring constantly. Stir in the wine. Boil until the liquid evaporates. Remove from the heat. Add the bread cubes and almonds and stir until combined.

- Spoon into a buttered baking dish and drizzle evenly with the stock. Bake at 350 degrees for 30 minutes or until heated through.

Serves 6 to 8

Grits Gnocchi à la Romaine

4	cups milk	1/8	teaspoon pepper
1/2	cup (1 stick) butter, cut into pieces	1/3	cup butter, melted
1	cup hominy grits (do not use quick-cooking grits)	4	ounces Gruyère cheese, shredded
1	teaspoon salt	1/3	cup freshly grated Parmesan cheese

- Bring the milk to a boil in a saucepan. Add 1/2 cup butter. Add the grits gradually, stirring constantly until combined. Bring to a boil and cook until the grits take on the appearance of a hot cooked breakfast cereal, stirring constantly. Remove from the heat. Season with the salt and pepper.

- Spoon into a mixing bowl and beat on high speed for 5 minutes or until creamy. Spoon into a 9×13-inch baking dish and let stand until set. Cut into rectangles and arrange, overlapping, in a buttered shallow decorative baking dish.

- Drizzle with 1/3 cup melted butter and sprinkle with the Gruyère cheese and Parmesan cheese. Bake at 400 degrees for 30 to 35 minutes.

Serves 6 to 8

Confetti Grits

1 cup yellow stone-ground grits or quick cooking grits
4 cups chicken broth
1 cup finely chopped yellow bell pepper
1/2 cup finely chopped red bell pepper
1/2 cup finely chopped red onion
6 ounces sharp Cheddar cheese, shredded
Cream (optional)

- Cook the grits according to the package directions, using broth for the water. Add the bell peppers and onion and cook for 5 minutes, stirring frequently. Add the cheese and stir until melted. Stir in enough cream to make the desired consistency.

Serves 6

Note: Pair this dish with any meat, any fish or barbecued shrimp. Tying this recipe to a bag of stone-ground grits makes a nice gift.

Lemon Rice

5 cups chicken broth
2 teaspoons minced garlic
2 cups long grain rice
1/4 cup lemon juice

2 tablespoons grated
   lemon zest
1/4 cup (1/2 stick) butter
   Salt and freshly ground
   pepper to taste

- Bring the broth and garlic to a boil in a saucepan.
- Stir in the rice and lemon juice. Simmer, covered, for 20 minutes. Remove from the heat.
- Stir in the lemon zest and let stand, covered, for 5 minutes.
- Add the butter and gently stir until melted. Season with salt and pepper.

Serves 8

Note: Serve this dish with Grilled Chicken with Soy Vinaigrette (page 132). To prepare Steamed Rice, combine 1 cup washed white rice, 1 1/2 cups boiling water and 1 teaspoon salt in a greased top of a double boiler. Cook over boiling water for 40 minutes or until the liquid is absorbed. Drizzle with 3 tablespoons melted butter.

Raja Rice Dish

1 cup chopped celery
3/4 cup chopped onion
6 tablespoons butter
3 cups chicken broth
2 cups white wine
1/4 cup chutney

   Salt and freshly ground
   pepper to taste
2 cups uncooked long grain
   white rice
1 cup chopped cashews

- Sauté the celery and onion in the butter in a skillet until onion is translucent.
- Stir in the broth, wine, chutney, salt and pepper. Bring to a boil.
- Spread the rice evenly in a greased 9x12-inch baking dish. Sprinkle with the cashews. Pour in the broth mixture and cover tightly with foil.
- Bake at 350 degrees for 45 to 60 minutes or until the liquid is absorbed.

Serves 8

Caribbean Sweet Rice

2	cups cooked white or brown rice	1/2	cup slivered almonds, toasted or Macadamia nuts, chopped
1	(11-ounce) can mandarin oranges, drained and chopped	1/4	cup flaked coconut, toasted
1	(8-ounce) can crushed pineapple, drained	3	tablespoons hot mango chutney
1/2	cup chopped red bell pepper	1	to 2 teaspoons fresh lime juice
1/3	cup sliced green onions	1/2	teaspoon grated fresh ginger

■ Cook the rice, mandarin oranges, pineapple, bell pepper, green onions, almonds, coconut, chutney, lime juice and ginger in a large skillet over medium-high heat, stirring constantly for 5 minutes or until heated through.

Serves 4

Nutty Wild Rice

4	cups (or more) chicken stock	2	onions, chopped
1	pound wild rice, rinsed and drained	2	tablespoons chopped parsley
4	ounces pine nuts or pecans	2	tablespoons golden raisins
2	tablespoons butter		Salt and freshly ground pepper

■ Bring the stock to a boil. Stir in the wild rice. Cook for 1 hour or until tender, adding additional stock as needed; drain.

■ Sauté the pine nuts in butter in a skillet until golden brown. Remove the pine nuts, reserving the pan drippings in the skillet.

■ Add the onions to the skillet and sauté in the pan drippings until translucent.

■ Add the parsley and raisins and sauté for 1 minute. Remove from the heat.

■ Combine the rice, pine nuts and onion mixture in a serving bowl and toss until combined. Season with salt and pepper.

Serves 8

Note: This dish has a wonderful nutty flavor. Pair this dish with game, turkey and all your holiday cooking.

Pesto Rice Timbales

1   red bell pepper, chopped
2   cups lightly packed fresh basil leaves
1   tablespoon water
1   cup long grain white rice
2   teaspoons vegetable oil
1   onion, finely chopped
1   large garlic clove, minced
1 3/4 cups chicken broth
1/2   teaspoon dried oregano
1/2   cup pine nuts, toasted (optional)
1/4   cup finely chopped fresh parsley
     Salt and pepper to taste
     Sprigs of basil

- Sprinkle 1/2 tablespoon chopped bell pepper into each of six 1/2-cup custard cups or ramekins.
- Process the basil and water in a food processor with a steel blade until puréed.
- Sauté the rice in oil in a saucepan over medium heat for 4 minutes or until golden brown.
- Add the onion and garlic and sauté for 1 minute.
- Add the remaining bell pepper, broth and oregano and bring to a boil, stirring occasionally.
- Reduce the heat to low and cook, covered, for 15 minutes or until the rice is tender and the liquid is absorbed. Remove from the heat and let stand, covered, for 10 minutes.
- Stir in the basil purée, pine nuts and parsley. Season with salt and pepper.
- Spoon the rice mixture into each custard cup, packing firmly.
- Unmold onto dinner plates and garnish with basil sprigs.

Serve 6

Variation: This dish can also be prepared in a large baking dish. Sprinkle the chopped bell pepper on top.

Chinese Vegetable Risotto

4 ounces dried mushrooms
2 1/2 cups chicken stock
1 1/2 cups arborio rice, rinsed and drained
1 teaspoon salt, or to taste
2 cups chopped onions
2 tablespoons olive oil
1/2 cup sliced carrots
1 cup sugar snap peas, strings removed
1/2 cup freshly grated Parmesan cheese
1 tablespoon olive oil
1 roasted Chinese red pepper, chopped (about 1 1/2 cups)
   (*see Note page 19*)

■ Rinse the mushrooms under cold water. Combine with enough hot water to cover in a bowl. Let stand for 30 minutes or until soft.

■ Drain and squeeze the mushrooms, reserving the liquid.

■ Remove and chop the mushroom stems. Chop the mushroom caps and set aside separately.

■ Combine the mushroom stems and the mushroom liquid in a saucepan and cook until the liquid is reduced to 1 tablespoon. Drain and reserve the liquid, discarding the stems.

■ Combine the mushroom liquid, stock and rice in a saucepan. Bring to a boil over high heat. Add salt. Reduce the heat to low and simmer, covered, for 25 minutes or until the water evaporates. Remove from the heat and let stand for 30 minutes.

■ Stir-fry the onions in 2 tablespoons olive oil in a wok until golden brown.

■ Add the mushroom caps and carrots and stir-fry until the carrots are tender.

■ Add the sugar snap peas and stir-fry for 1 minute. Turn off the heat.

■ Add the cooked rice and mix well.

■ Sprinkle with the cheese and drizzle with the olive oil; mix until combined.

■ Stir in the Chinese red pepper. Serve at room temperature.

Serves 4

Risotto with Spinach, Fontina and Prosciutto

1^1/2 cups chicken stock
2   cups water
1   small onion, minced
1   tablespoon olive oil
1   cup arborio rice
^{1}/2 cup white wine
4   ounces frozen spinach, thawed and squeezed dry
4   ounces fontina cheese, shredded
3   ounces thinly sliced prosciutto, cut horizontally into ^{1}/2-inch strips
    Freshly ground pepper to taste

- Simmer the stock and water in a saucepan; keep warm.

- Sauté the onion in the olive oil in a skillet for 3 minutes or until translucent.

- Add the rice and sauté for 1 minute or until evenly coated with the oil.

- Add the wine and cook over medium-high heat for 2 minutes or until reduced to ^{1}/4 cup.

- Add the stock mixture to the rice ^{1}/2 cup at a time, simmering until the liquid is almost absorbed before adding the next addition, stirring constantly. The rice should be creamy and tender.

- Stir in the spinach and cook for 2 minutes or until heated through. Remove from the heat.

- Stir in the cheese and prosciutto and season with pepper. Serve immediately.

Serves 4

Variation: You may substitute Parmesan cheese for the fontina cheese and ham for the prosciutto, if desired.

Lemon Pasta with Pine Nuts

3	tablespoons minced garlic		Salt and freshly ground
1/2	cup extra-virgin olive oil		pepper to taste
1	cup minced flat-leaf parsley	1	pound angel hair pasta,
1/2	cup toasted pine nuts,		vermicelli or cappellini
	slightly crushed		Freshly grated Parmesan
1/2	cup lemon juice		cheese
2	tablespoons grated lemon zest		

- Sauté the garlic in the olive oil until soft. Spoon into a large bowl. Add the parsley, pine nuts, lemon juice, lemon zest, salt and pepper.
- Cook the pasta according to the package directions. Drain, reserving some of the liquid. Add the pasta to the garlic mixture and toss until combined.
- Add enough cooking liquid gradually to moisten the pasta. Sprinkle with the cheese just before serving.

Serves 8

Variation: You may add steamed vegetables and red pepper flakes for a kick.

Summer Pasta

4	tomatoes, peeled, seeded and chopped	2	garlic cloves, minced
			Salt and pepper to taste
16	ounces mozzarella cheese, chopped	1	pound spaghetti
			Freshly grated Parmesan
1	cup olive oil		cheese
1/4	cup minced fresh basil		

- Combine the tomatoes, mozzarella cheese, olive oil, basil, garlic, salt and pepper in a bowl. Let stand at room temperature.
- Cook the pasta according to the package directions.
- Add the tomato mixture to the hot pasta in a large bowl and toss until combined. Sprinkle with Parmesan cheese.

Serves 4 to 6

Variation: To serve as a one-dish meal, toss in 1 pound peeled cooked small shrimp just before serving.

Little Italy Spaghetti

1	(13-ounce) package spaghetti or pasta of your choice	1	tablespoon red pepper flakes
6	to 8 ounces pancetta, chopped	1	(15-ounce) can diced tomatoes
3	tablespoons extra-virgin olive oil	1	or 2 garlic cloves, minced
1	red onion, chopped	3/4	cup freshly grated pecorino Romano cheese
			Slivered fresh basil

- Cook the pasta according to the package directions; drain.

- Cook the pancetta in the olive oil in a skillet over medium-high heat until crisp.

- Add the onion and red pepper flakes and cook until the onions are tender, stirring occasionally. Stir in the tomatoes and garlic.

- Add the pasta and toss until evenly coated. Cook for 5 minutes or until the pasta is lightly toasted. Toss again and cook for 5 minutes.

- Divide among six plates or pasta bowls. Sprinkle with the cheese and slivered basil.

Serves 6

Vodka Pasta Presto

1	pound miniature penne pasta	1/4	teaspoon salt
16	cups boiling water	5	ounces Herb Cheese Spread (*page 31*)
1	to 2 tablespoons salt		
2	(15- to 16-ounce) cans whole tomatoes in purée	1/3	cup vodka
		1/3	cup thinly sliced basil
1/4	teaspoon freshly ground pepper	1/4	teaspoon freshly ground pepper

- Cook the pasta in the boiling water with 1 to 2 tablespoons salt. Drain, reserving 1/2 cup of the liquid.

- Chop the tomatoes. Combine the undrained tomatoes, 1/4 teaspoon pepper and 1/4 teaspoon salt in a saucepan and bring to a boil. Reduce the heat to medium and simmer, covered, for 6 minutes. Stir in the Herb Cheese Spread and vodka and cook until the cheese is melted.

- Combine the pasta, 1/2 cup reserved pasta cooking liquid, half the tomato mixture and the basil in a serving bowl and toss until combined. Spoon the remaining sauce on top and sprinkle with 1/4 teaspoon pepper.

Serves 4

Bow Tie Pasta with Sun-Dried Tomato Sauce

12   ounces Brie cheese
1   (8-ounce) jar oil-pack sun-dried tomatoes
1   cup kalamata olives,
      cut into halves
1   cup slivered basil
1/2   cup grated lemon zest
1/2   cup olive oil
2   garlic cloves, minced
2   teaspoons pepper
1   pound bow tie pasta

- Freeze the cheese, covered, for 1 hour. Cut off and discard the rind and shred the frozen cheese with a hand-held cheese slicer.

- Drain and chop the sun-dried tomatoes, reserving 1/4 cup of the oil.

- Combine the shredded cheese, sun-dried tomatoes, reserved sun-dried tomato oil, olives, basil, lemon zest, olive oil, garlic and pepper in a bowl and mix well. Let stand, covered, at room temperature for 4 hours.

- Cook the pasta according to the package directions; drain.

- Add the pasta to the sun-dried tomato mixture, tossing until combined. Serve immediately.

Serves 6

Note: To add a smoky flavor to any pasta sauce, drizzle vegetables with good-quality olive oil and season with salt and pepper. Bake at 250 degrees for 1 hour or until the vegetables begin to blacken.

Family Barbecue

Barren roadside tables become full of life and color with the summer solstice. Everyone tries his or her hand as a farmer. Fresh fish and seafood are caught right out of the back door from either the Atlantic Ocean or Cape Fear River, and local produce provides wonderful greens and berries.

BLT New Potatoes
Italian Baked Oysters with Toasted Pita Chips

Broiled Deviled Hamburgers with Picadilla Sauce
Barbecued Franks
Carolina Baby Back Ribs
Coleslaw
South-of-the-Border Black Bean Salad

Banana Pudding Extravaganza

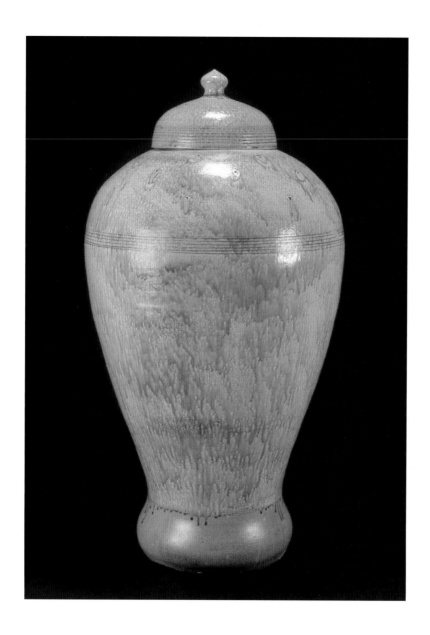

Mark Hewitt (English, 1955)
Yellow Dog, 2001
Wood-fired, salt-glazed stoneware, alkaline glaze with blue glass on shoulders
Purchased from the artist with funds from the Claude Howell Endowment
for the Purchase of North Carolina Art
Photograph by Jackson Smith

Brunch

The Cook's Canvas 2

Front Street Chipped Beef

1   pound chipped beef, cut into $1/2$-inch strips
1/4 cup ($1/2$ stick) butter
1   pound mushrooms, sliced
1/2 cup minced onion
1/2 cup all-purpose flour
3   cups light cream
2   cups milk
2   (14-ounce) cans artichoke hearts, drained and cut into quarters
3   tablespoons capers, drained
3   tablespoons prepared horseradish
    Salt and freshly ground pepper to taste
1   (14-ounce) can pitted black olives, drained
6   English muffins, split and toasted

- Soak the chipped beef in enough hot water to cover in a bowl for 30 minutes; drain.

- Melt 2 tablespoons of the butter in a large skillet and add the chipped beef, mushrooms and onion. Cook for 3 minutes or until the beef begins to curl.

- Add the remaining 2 tablespoons butter. Stir in the flour to make a roux. Cook for 2 minutes, stirring constantly. Mix in the cream and milk.

- Cook until thickened, stirring constantly. Add the artichoke hearts, capers, prepared horseradish, salt and pepper. Spoon the chipped beef mixture into a chafing dish or serving dish and sprinkle with the olives.

- Serve warm over the muffin halves.

Serves 12

Note: *Chipped beef has faded from the scene. This version is "comfort food" with a new twist. Serve with Hot Fruit (page 219).*

Cold Ham Mousse

1 tablespoon plus 1 teaspoon unflavored gelatin	1/4 cup mayonnaise
1/4 cup dry white wine	2 teaspoons Dijon mustard
2 tablespoons butter	1/2 cup heavy whipping cream, whipped
1 tablespoon all-purpose flour	Lettuce leaves
1 cup half-and-half	Parsley Sauce (*below*)
2 1/2 cups finely ground ham	

- Soften the gelatin in the wine in a small bowl.
- Melt the butter in a saucepan and stir in the flour to make a roux. Cook until smooth and bubbly.
- Add the half-and-half and cook over low heat until thickened, stirring constantly. Stir in the gelatin mixture and let stand until cool.
- Combine the ham, mayonnaise and Dijon mustard in a bowl and mix well. Stir into the gelatin mixture. Chill, covered, in the refrigerator until partially set. Fold in the whipped cream.
- Coat a 1 1/2-quart mold with additional mayonnaise or nonstick cooking spray. Spoon the ham mixture into the prepared mold and chill until set.
- Unmold onto a chilled serving platter and surround with lettuce leaves. Serve with the Parsley Sauce.

Serves 6 to 8

Parsley Sauce

1 cup sour cream	1 garlic clove, crushed
1/2 cup mayonnaise	Salt and freshly ground pepper to taste
3/4 cup finely chopped parsley	
2 teaspoons finely chopped onion	

- Combine the sour cream and mayonnaise in a bowl. Stir in the parsley, onion, garlic, salt and pepper.
- Chill, covered, in the refrigerator.

Makes 2 cups

Variation: *You may substitute spinach or watercress for the parsley.*

Ham Soufflé with Mushroom Sauce

2½ pounds ground ham
2½ pounds sharp Cheddar cheese, shredded
15   eggs, beaten
2½ quarts (10 cups) milk
8   ounces unsalted soda crackers, crumbled
2   garlic cloves, minced, or to taste
½ teaspoon baking soda
      Tabasco sauce to taste
      Mushroom Sauce (below)

■ Combine the ground ham, cheese and eggs in a large bowl and mix well. Add the milk, cracker crumbs, garlic, baking soda and Tabasco sauce and mix well.

■ Spoon the ham mixture evenly into two greased 9×13-inch baking pans.

■ Bake at 350 degrees for 2 hours, switching the position of the pans after 1 hour.

■ Serve with the Mushroom Sauce.

Serves 24

Note: *Great for a crowd and easy to make.*

Mushroom Sauce

2   pounds assorted mushrooms, trimmed and sliced
½ cup (1 stick) butter
2   tablespoons all-purpose flour
1½ cups chicken broth
2   cups sour cream

■ Sauté the mushrooms in the butter in a large skillet.

■ Stir in the flour to make a roux. Add the broth gradually, stirring constantly.

■ Cook until thickened, stirring constantly. Fold in the sour cream.

Makes 6 cups

Sausage and Bell Peppers with Parmesan Cheese Grits

19	ounces sweet Italian-style sausage, casings removed	1	large sweet onion, cut into halves and thinly sliced
1	yellow bell pepper, cut into thin strips	1	to 2 teaspoons Italian seasoning
1	red bell pepper, cut into thin strips	1	teaspoon salt
1	green bell pepper, cut into thin strips	1/2	teaspoon freshly ground pepper
2	garlic cloves, minced		Parmesan Cheese Grits (below) Freshly grated Parmesan cheese

■ Cook the sausage with the bell peppers, garlic, onion, Italian seasoning, salt and pepper in a large skillet over medium high heat, stirring until the sausage is crumbly and the vegetables are tender.

■ Spoon the sausage mixture over the Parmesan Cheese Grits and garnish with Parmesan cheese.

Serves 4

Parmesan Cheese Grits

1 cup grits
4 cups milk
1 1/4 cups freshly grated Parmesan cheese
1 tablespoon butter
3/4 teaspoon salt

■ Cook the grits using the package directions, substituting the milk for the liquid. Stir in the cheese, butter and salt.

Serves 4

Note: Grits are a southern staple. To add more flavor, cook grits in chicken stock or milk. Vary the flavor by adding Boursin, Cheddar cheese, or Saga blue cheese. You may prepare in advance. Spread in a shallow dish, and chill, covered, in the refrigerator. Cut the grits into squares and arrange on an ovenproof platter. Bake at 350 degrees until hot.

Sausage and Grits Casserole

1   cup grits (3 cups cooked)
    Milk
8   ounces hot bulk pork sausage
8   ounces mild bulk pork sausage
10 ounces sharp Cheddar cheese, shredded
1³/4 cups milk
3   eggs, beaten
3   tablespoons butter, melted

- Cook the grits according to the package directions, using half water and half milk for the liquid.
- Brown the hot and mild sausages in a skillet, stirring until crumbly; drain. Combine the sausage, grits, cheese, 1³/4 cups milk, the eggs and butter in a bowl and mix well.
- Spoon the sausage mixture into an ungreased baking dish. Bake at 350 degrees for 1 hour.

Serves 8

Note: You may bake for 30 to 45 minutes and then freeze for future use. Thaw in the refrigerator and bake at 350 degrees for 15 minutes or until heated through. Serve with Cinnamon Red Apples (page 220) and toast. A great Christmas morning dish.

Mediterranean Chicken and Orzo Salad

10 ounces grape tomatoes or cherry tomatoes,
    cut into quarters (about 2 cups)
12 kalamata olives, coarsely chopped
1/4 cup snipped fresh parsley
2   tablespoons capers, drained and rinsed
2   tablespoons red wine vinegar
2   teaspoons extra-virgin olive oil
1 1/2 teaspoons snipped fresh basil
1   teaspoon vegetable oil
1   pound boneless skinless chicken breasts, sliced
1   (14-ounce) can chicken broth
1   cup orzo pasta
1/2 teaspoon snipped fresh basil
3   ounces feta cheese, crumbled

- Combine the tomatoes, olives, parsley, capers, vinegar, olive oil and 1 1/2 teaspoons basil in a bowl. Toss gently until the vegetables are coated.

- Heat a 12-inch skillet over medium-high heat. Remove from the heat and add the vegetable oil to the hot skillet. Swirl to ensure even coverage. Return to the heat and add the chicken.

- Cook for 2 minutes on each side or until light brown. Remove the chicken to a platter, reserving the pan drippings.

- Add the broth and pasta to the reserved pan drippings and increase the heat to high. Bring to a boil, scraping any brown bits from the bottom of the skillet with a wooden spoon.

- Arrange the chicken over the pasta and sprinkle with 1/2 teaspoon basil. Reduce the heat to low and simmer, covered, for 12 minutes or until the chicken is cooked through and the pasta is al dente, stirring occasionally.

- Spoon the pasta onto a serving platter and top with the chicken. Spoon the vegetable mixture over the chicken. Sprinkle with the cheese.

Serves 4

Note: Wonderful served with a green salad and crusty bread.

Pastry-Wrapped Cheesy Chicken

1   (17-ounce) package frozen puff pastry sheets, thawed
4   ounces Herb Cheese Spread (*page 31*)
6   boneless skinless chicken breasts
1/2   teaspoon salt
1/8   teaspoon freshly ground pepper
1   egg, beaten
1   tablespoon water

- Unfold the pastry sheets on a lightly floured surface. Roll each sheet into a 12×14-inch rectangle with a rolling pin. Cut one sheet into four 6×7-inch rectangles. Cut the remaining sheet into two 6×7-inch rectangles and one 6×12-inch rectangle.

- Shape the small rectangles into ovals by trimming the corners. Spread the Herb Cheese Spread over the ovals to within 1/4 inch of edges.

- Sprinkle the chicken with the salt and pepper and place one chicken breast in the center of each oval. Moisten the edges of the ovals with water and fold end over end and side over side to enclose the filling; press to seal.

- Arrange bundles seam side down on a lightly greased baking sheet.

- Cut the remaining 6×12-inch rectangle into twelve 1/2-inch strips. Braid the strips two at a time and arrange lengthwise over the bundles. Chill, covered, for 2 hours, if desired.

- Whisk the egg and water in a bowl until blended and brush over the top of the bundles.

- Bake at 400 degrees for 25 to 30 minutes or until the chicken is cooked through and the pastry is light brown.

Serves 6

Crab on English

1/2 cup (1 stick) butter
3/4 cup finely minced celery
3 tablespoons (or more) prepared horseradish
1 teaspoon minced garlic
3 tablespoons all-purpose flour
3 tablespoons lemon juice
3 tablespoons water
2 teaspoons Worcestershire sauce
16 ounces cream cheese, cubed and softened
2 cups sour cream
1 cup mayonnaise
1/2 teaspoon salt
1/2 teaspoon freshly ground pepper
1/4 cup freshly grated Romano cheese or Parmesan cheese
1 pound fresh crab meat (*see Note page 22*)
6 English muffins, split and lightly toasted

▪ Melt the butter in a saucepan. Add the celery, prepared horseradish and garlic. Cook until the celery is tender but not brown.

▪ Add the flour and mix until combined. Stir in the lemon juice, water and Worcestershire sauce. Cook over low heat until thickened, stirring constantly.

▪ Remove from the heat and mix in the cream cheese. Stir in the sour cream, mayonnaise, salt and pepper. Fold in the Romano or Parmesan cheese and crab meat.

▪ Spread the crab meat mixture on the cut sides of the muffins and arrange crab side up on a baking sheet. Broil until heated through.

Serves 6

Note: This crab dip can also be served in greased individual ramekins. Bake at 350 degrees for 20 minutes. Serve with garlic bread. For an appetizer, bake in a baking dish at 350 degrees until hot and serve with garlic bread or Crostini (page 69).

Southern-Style Crab Cakes

1 pound white crab meat (*see Note page 22*)	1/3 cup mayonnaise
1/2 red bell pepper, minced	1/4 cup whole grain mustard
1/2 yellow bell pepper, minced	1/4 cup lemon juice
1/2 onion, minced	1 tablespoon freshly ground pepper
1/2 bunch green onions, trimmed and minced	Pecan Tartar Sauce (*below*) or Low-Country Tartar Sauce (*page 209*)
3 ribs celery, minced	
3 cups herb-seasoned stuffing mix	

- Combine the crab meat, bell peppers, onion, green onions and celery in a bowl and mix well. Stir in the stuffing mix and let stand for 10 minutes.

- Combine the mayonnaise, whole grain mustard, lemon juice and pepper in a bowl and mix well. Stir into the crab meat mixture. Shape the crab meat mixture into eight cakes and arrange in a single layer in a baking pan sprayed with nonstick cooking spray. Bake at 350 degrees for 10 minutes. Increase the oven temperature to 450 degrees and bake for 10 minutes longer or until brown. Serve warm with the Pecan Tartar Sauce or Low-Country Tartar Sauce.

Makes 8 crab cakes

Pecan Tartar Sauce

1/2 cup coarsely chopped pecans, toasted	1 tablespoon minced pickles or cornichons
1/2 cup mayonnaise	1 teaspoon minced lemon zest
1 tablespoon cider vinegar	1/2 teaspoon dry mustard
1 tablespoon minced fresh parsley	1/4 teaspoon salt

- Combine the pecans, mayonnaise, vinegar, parsley, pickles, lemon zest, dry mustard and salt in a bowl and mix well.

- Store, covered, in the refrigerator.

Makes 1 cup

Note: You may also serve with crab or shrimp or as a new twist for any fish.

Low-Country Tartar Sauce

1	red bell pepper, coarsely chopped	1/2	bunch green onion tops, finely sliced
1	small onion, coarsely chopped	1 1/2	cups mayonnaise
1	tablespoon lemon juice	1	tablespoon Cajun spice
1/2	teaspoon chopped garlic	1	tablespoon salt
		1	tablespoon freshly ground pepper

- Combine the bell pepper, onion, lemon juice and garlic in a food processor fitted with a steel blade. Pulse until the vegetables are finely chopped but not puréed.
- Combine the green onion tops, mayonnaise, Cajun spice, salt and pepper in a bowl and mix well. Stir in the bell pepper mixture.
- Store, covered, in the refrigerator.

Makes 2 cups

Note: *Great with seafood or steak or on ham sandwiches.*

Bank's Channel Crab Casserole

2	cups seasoned croutons	1	pound fresh crab meat (*see Note page* 22)
1	cup chopped celery		
1/2	cup chopped onion	1/2	cup freshly grated Parmesan cheese
1	cup mayonnaise		
	Juice of 1 lemon	1/2	cup (1 stick) butter, softened
	Dash of hot red pepper sauce	1/2	cup fine bread crumbs
	Salt and freshly ground pepper to taste		

- Combine the croutons, celery, onion, mayonnaise, lemon juice, hot sauce, salt and pepper in a bowl and mix well. Fold in the crab meat and spoon into a 2-quart baking dish.
- Mix the cheese, butter and bread crumbs in a bowl until crumbly. Sprinkle the crumb mixture over the crab meat mixture.
- Bake at 350 degrees for 50 to 60 minutes or until brown and bubbly.

Serves 6

Crab Brunch Squares with
Red Bell Pepper Cream Sauce

2²/3 cups milk
4 eggs
3/4 teaspoon Dijon mustard
6 ounces Brie cheese, rind removed and cut into 1/4-inch cubes
1/2 cup sliced black olives
1 small onion, finely chopped
1 teaspoon Worcestershire sauce

1 pound crab meat (see Note page 22)
3¹/2 cups cooked rice
2 tablespoons chopped fresh chives
Paprika to taste
Red Bell Pepper Cream Sauce (below)

■ Whisk the milk, eggs and Dijon mustard in a bowl until blended. Stir in the cheese, olives, onion and Worcestershire sauce. Add the crab meat and rice; mix gently.

■ Spoon into a greased 9×13-inch baking dish and bake at 350 degrees for 40 to 45 minutes or until a knife inserted in the center comes out clean.

■ Cut into squares and sprinkle with the chives and paprika. Serve with the Red Bell Pepper Cream Sauce.

Serves 8

Red Bell Pepper Cream Sauce

1 large red bell pepper, chopped
1 green onion, sliced
1/4 cup (1/2 stick) unsalted butter
1/4 cup all-purpose flour

Salt and freshly ground pepper to taste
1³/4 cups milk
1 tablespoon lemon juice

■ Sauté the bell pepper and green onion in the butter in a skillet for 2 minutes. Reduce the heat to low and mix in the flour. Cook for 3 minutes, stirring frequently. Season with salt and pepper.

■ Whisk in the milk and lemon juice gradually and cook until thickened. Process the sauce in a blender for 2 minutes or until puréed. Return the purée to the saucepan and keep warm over low heat.

Makes 3 cups

Shrimp and Wild Rice Casserole

4   cups water
2   tablespoons salt
1 1/2 pounds shrimp
1   (6-ounce) package long grain and wild rice mix
3   tablespoons butter
3/4 cup sliced celery
1/2 cup chopped onion
1/2 cup chopped green bell pepper
1   garlic clove, minced
3   tablespoons all-purpose flour
3/4 teaspoon salt
1/2 teaspoon freshly ground pepper
1   cup milk
1/2 cup chicken broth
1   cup fresh mushrooms, sliced
1/3 cup sliced almonds, toasted

- Bring the water and salt to a boil in a stockpot and add the shrimp. Boil for 30 seconds and drain. Rinse the shrimp under cold water for 1 to 2 minutes. Peel and devein the shrimp.

- Cook the rice using the package directions.

- Melt the butter in a skillet and add the celery, onion, bell pepper and garlic. Cook until tender but not brown. Add the flour, salt and pepper to make a roux. Mix well.

- Add the milk and broth gradually, stirring constantly. Cook until thickened, stirring frequently. Add the shrimp, rice, mushrooms and almonds; mix gently.

- Spoon the shrimp mixture into a greased 2-quart baking dish. Bake at 425 degrees for 20 to 25 minutes or until bubbly and heated through.

Serves 6

Baked Asparagus with Cheese

1	pound fresh asparagus	1¹/2	teaspoons salt
12	slices French bread	¹/4	teaspoon ground nutmeg
12	ounces Gruyère cheese, grated		Freshly ground pepper
2¹/4	cups milk		to taste
4	eggs	2	ounces sharp Cheddar
1	tablespoon chopped onion		cheese, shredded

- Snap off the thick woody ends of the asparagus spears and discard. Cut the asparagus into bite-size pieces.

- Layer the bread slices, Gruyère cheese and asparagus one-half at a time in a 9×13-inch baking dish.

- Whisk the milk, eggs, onion, salt, nutmeg and pepper in a bowl until combined. Pour over the prepared layers.

- Bake at 350 degrees for 25 minutes. Sprinkle with the Cheddar cheese and bake for 10 minutes longer.

Serves 6

Artichoke and Avocado Quiche

1	avocado	1	(9-inch) pie shell,
3	tablespoons lemon juice		partially baked
1	cup whipping cream	¹/2	cup (2 ounces) grated
3	eggs		Gruyère cheese
	Salt and freshly ground		Avocado slices
	pepper to taste		Chopped parsley
1	(14-ounce) can artichoke		Paprika
	hearts, drained and quartered		

- Slice the avocado and drizzle with the lemon juice to prevent browning.

- Whisk the cream, eggs, salt and pepper in a bowl. Fold in the avocado and artichoke hearts.

- Pour the artichoke mixture into the pie shell and sprinkle with the cheese.

- Bake at 375 degrees for 25 to 30 minutes or until set, puffed and brown. Cut into wedges. Garnish with avocado slices, parsley and paprika.

Serves 6 to 8

Green Onion and Red Bell Pepper Tart

1¹/2 teaspoons butter
¹/4 cup pine nuts
3 tablespoons butter
1 large red bell pepper, chopped
2 teaspoons sugar
2 teaspoons red wine vinegar
2 bunches green onions, chopped
1¹/2 tablespoons unbleached all-purpose flour
²/3 cup half-and-half
3 egg yolks

2 egg whites
1 tablespoon chopped fresh dill weed, or 1 teaspoon dried dill weed
¹/2 teaspoon salt
Freshly ground pepper to taste
1 unbaked refrigerator pie pastry
1¹/2 teaspoons Dijon mustard
4 ounces goat cheese, crumbled

- Melt 1¹/2 teaspoons butter in a skillet over medium heat and stir in the pine nuts. Cook for 4 minutes or until light brown. Remove the pine nuts to a platter to cool using a slotted spoon, reserving the pan drippings.

- Melt 3 tablespoons butter with the reserved pan drippings and add the bell pepper. Cook for 4 minutes or until tender. Stir in the sugar and vinegar and cook for 1¹/2 minutes or until of a syrup consistency.

- Add the green onions and flour and mix well. Cook for 1 minute or until the green onions are tender.

- Combine the half-and-half, egg yolks, egg whites, dill weed, salt and pepper in a food processor fitted with a steel blade. Process until blended.

- Line a French tart pan with the pastry. Spread the Dijon mustard over the bottom of the pastry. Spread the bell pepper mixture in the pastry-lined tart pan. Pour the half-and-half mixture evenly over the vegetables. Sprinkle with the cheese.

- Place the tart pan on a baking sheet and bake at 375 degrees for 35 minutes. Sprinkle with the pine nuts and bake for 10 minutes longer or until puffed and brown.

Serves 6

Note: This tart can be cut into squares and served as an appetizer.

Tomato Pie

1 unbaked refrigerator pie pastry
2 cups fresh spinach, stems removed
1/2 sweet onion, thinly sliced
5 ripe tomatoes, sliced
1 cup mayonnaise

1 cup freshly grated Parmesan cheese
Splash of Worcestershire sauce
Dash of hot red pepper sauce
Freshly ground pepper to taste

- Fit the pastry into a pie plate and flute the edge. Prick the bottom of the pastry with a fork. Bake at 350 degrees for 5 minutes. Maintain the oven temperature.

- Layer the spinach, onion and tomatoes in the pastry-lined pie plate.

- Mix the mayonnaise, cheese, Worcestershire sauce, hot sauce and pepper in a bowl and spread over the prepared layers.

- Bake for 30 minutes. Serve warm or chilled.

Serves 6

Note: *This can also be made successfully without the crust.*

Monterey Eggs

1 (4-ounce) can diced green chiles, drained
2 cups half-and-half
9 eggs, beaten
1/3 cup mixed chopped fresh chives, parsley and thyme

Salt and freshly ground pepper to taste
6 tomato slices
6 tablespoons freshly grated Parmesan cheese
6 thin avocado wedges
6 sprigs of parsley

- Divide the chiles evenly among six ramekins sprayed with nonstick cooking spray.

- Whisk the half-and-half, eggs, chive mixture, salt and pepper in a bowl until mixed and pour evenly into the prepared ramekins.

- Bake at 325 degrees for 25 minutes or until set. Top each ramekin with one tomato slice and 1 tablespoon of the cheese.

- Broil until bubbly. Top each with one avocado wedge and one sprig of parsley.

Serves 6

Sausage and Cheese Strata with Sun-Dried Tomatoes

$1/2$ cup chopped sun-dried tomatoes
        (do not use oil-pack)
11   slices white sourdough sandwich bread
1   pound hot Italian sausage, casings removed
1   teaspoon butter
$3^1/2$ cups milk
8   eggs
2   teaspoons minced fresh thyme,
        or $3/4$ teaspoon dried thyme
$1^1/2$ teaspoons salt
$1/4$ teaspoon freshly ground pepper
$1/2$ cup chopped onion
$1/2$ cup grated Parmesan cheese
4   ounces mozzarella cheese, shredded
8   ounces (or more) soft fresh goat cheese, crumbled
        Chopped fresh parsley

- Pour enough boiling water over the sun-dried tomatoes to cover in a heatproof bowl. Let stand until softened; drain. Trim the crusts from the bread and discard. Cut the remaining bread into 1-inch pieces.

- Brown the sausage in a skillet over medium heat, stirring until crumbly; drain.

- Coat a 9×13-inch baking dish with the butter.

- Whisk the milk, eggs, thyme, salt and pepper in a bowl until combined. Add the sun-dried tomatoes, bread, sausage, onion and Parmesan cheese and mix well. Pour into the prepared baking dish and chill, covered, for 4 hours or longer.

- Bake at 375 degrees for 45 minutes or until puffed and golden brown. Sprinkle with the mozzarella cheese and goat cheese and bake for 5 minutes longer or until the cheese melts.

- Cool on a wire rack for 5 minutes. Sprinkle with parsley and serve.

Serves 8

French Toast Strata

1   (16-ounce) loaf French bread, cubed
8   ounces cream cheese, cubed
2 1/2 cups milk
8   eggs
1/2 cup (1 stick) butter, melted
1/4 cup maple syrup
    Cider Syrup (*below*)

- Layer half the bread, the cream cheese and the remaining bread in a greased 9×13-inch baking dish.
- Whisk the milk, eggs, butter and maple syrup in a bowl until blended. Pour over the prepared layers. Lightly press to ensure all the layers are immersed in the milk mixture.
- Chill, covered with plastic wrap, for 2 to 24 hours.
- Bake, covered with foil, at 325 degrees for 35 minutes. Remove the cover and bake for 15 minutes longer. Serve with the Cider Syrup.

Serves 8

Cider Syrup

1/2 cup sugar
4   teaspoons cornstarch
1/2 teaspoon cinnamon
1   cup apple juice or cider
1   tablespoon lemon juice
1   teaspoon butter

- Combine the sugar, cornstarch and cinnamon in a saucepan and mix well. Stir in the apple juice or cider and bring to a boil.
- Boil for 2 to 3 minutes and stir in the lemon juice and butter.

Makes 1 1/4 cups

Note: *Warm Cider Syrup is also good over pancakes or waffles.*

Apple Cinnamon French Toast

5 tablespoons butter
2 large baking apples, peeled and thinly sliced
1 cup packed dark brown sugar
2 tablespoons dark corn syrup
1 teaspoon cinnamon

8 (1-inch-thick) slices French bread
1 cup milk
3 eggs
1 teaspoon vanilla extract

- Melt the butter in a skillet and add the apples. Cook until the apples are tender-crisp. Stir in the brown sugar, corn syrup and cinnamon.
- Cook until the sugar dissolves and pour the apple mixture into a 9×13-inch baking pan. Arrange the bread slices in a single layer over the apple mixture.
- Whisk the milk, eggs and vanilla in a bowl until blended and pour over the prepared layers. Chill, covered, for 8 to 10 hours or overnight.
- Bake at 375 degrees for 30 to 35 minutes. Cool for 5 minutes and invert onto a serving platter.

Serves 6

Glazed Pineapple with Macadamia Nut Crunch

1 cup coarsely chopped macadamia nuts
1/3 cup packed light brown sugar
1/8 teaspoon salt

1/4 cup (1/2 stick) butter, melted
1 fresh pineapple, cut into 1-inch-thick slices

- Mix the macadamia nuts, brown sugar and salt in a bowl. Stir in the butter.
- Arrange the pineapple slices in a single layer on a baking sheet lined with foil. Spoon a few tablespoons of the macadamia nut mixture over each slice.
- Broil 6 inches from the heat source for 1 1/2 minutes or until the mixture begins to caramelize.

Serves 6

Note: Your house guests will love this for breakfast. Or, serve with a ham entrée for dinner. When buying fresh pineapple, pluck a leaf from the crown. If it pulls out easily, the fruit is ripe.

Victorian Inn Granola Yogurt Cups

    4   cups Granola (*below*)
    4   cups yogurt
    4   cups chopped seasonal fresh fruit

- Alternate layers of the Granola, yogurt and fruit in eight large red wine glasses, ending with the fruit.
- Serve at breakfast or for a buffet brunch.

Serves 8

Granola

    1¹/₂ cups rolled oats
    1   cup bran flakes
    ¹/₂ cup toasted sunflower seeds
    ¹/₂ cup sweetened flaked coconut
    ¹/₂ cup sliced almonds, toasted
    ¹/₂ cup wheat germ
    ¹/₄ cup sesame seeds

    ¹/₄ cup honey
    ¹/₄ cup vegetable oil
    1   teaspoon vanilla extract
    1   teaspoon almond extract
    ¹/₂ cup dried cranberries or
         golden raisins

- Mix the oats, bran flakes, sunflower seeds, coconut, almonds, wheat germ and sesame seeds in a large bowl.
- Heat the honey, oil and flavorings in a small saucepan; do not boil. Pour the warm honey mixture over the oat mixture and mix well.
- Spread the oat mixture in a uniform depth in a greased shallow baking pan. Bake at 300 degrees for 15 minutes, stirring every 5 minutes. Stir in the cranberries.
- Let stand until cool and store in an airtight container.

Makes 5 cups

Hot Fruit

1   (16-ounce) can apricots,
    drained
1   (16-ounce) can pears, drained
1   (16-ounce) can pitted black
    cherries, drained
1   (16-ounce) can pineapple
    chunks, drained
1   cup applesauce
1   (10-ounce) package frozen
    raspberries, thawed
1/4 cup honey
2   tablespoons frozen orange
    juice concentrate, thawed

■ Combine the apricots, pears, cherries, pineapple and applesauce in a bowl and
  mix well. Spoon the apricot mixture into a 2-quart baking dish and sprinkle with
  the raspberries.
■ Mix the honey and orange juice concentrate in a bowl and pour over the
  prepared layers.
■ Bake at 350 degrees for 20 minutes. Serve warm.

Serves 10

Vanilla-Poached Fruit

2   lemons
2   cups water
1/2 cup sugar
2   vanilla beans, split
4   pears, peeled and cut into
    quarters
4   Granny Smith apples, peeled
    and cut into quarters
1/2 cup dried cranberries
    Apple juice (optional)

■ Remove the zest from the lemons in long strips using a zester or vegetable peeler.
  Place the zest in a saucepan. Squeeze the lemons to release the juice into the
  saucepan. Add the water, sugar and vanilla beans and stir until the sugar dissolves.
  Bring to a boil and reduce the heat. Simmer for 5 minutes.
■ Arrange the pears and apples in a shallow baking dish and sprinkle with the
  cranberries. Pour the hot lemon mixture over the fruit. Add enough apple juice to
  cover the fruit if necessary. Bake at 375 degrees for 30 to 45 minutes or until
  the fruit is tender. Discard the vanilla beans and serve warm or chilled.

Serves 8

Note: *Good served with baked ham.*

Peppered Pears

4   Bosc pears or other firm pears, peeled and cut into halves
2   teaspoons freshly ground pepper
2   teaspoons sugar
1/2 cup dry white wine
1¹/2 tablespoons butter

■ Arrange the pears cut side down in a baking dish and sprinkle with the pepper and sugar. Pour the wine over the pears and dot with the butter.

■ Bake, covered, at 350 degrees for 30 to 45 minutes or until fork tender. Remove the cover and bake for 15 minutes longer.

■ Cool the pears in the liquid. Chill, covered, for several hours.

■ Cut the pears into halves before serving.

Makes 16 pear quarters

Note: *Serve with a deli tray of cold meats, as a delicious accompaniment to pâtés, or, thinly sliced, as a wonderful addition to a ham sandwich.*

Cinnamon Red Apples

1   cup water
1   cup sugar
1/3 cup red hot cinnamon candies
6   apples, peeled, cored and sliced into rings (Gala, Fuji or Roma)
     Dash of salt

■ Combine the water, sugar and candies in a saucepan and cook for 10 minutes or until the candies dissolve. Add the apples and salt and mix well.

■ Simmer for 15 minutes or until the apples are tender. Remove from the heat and let the apples stand in the syrup until partially cool. Remove the apples to a serving dish using a slotted spoon, reserving the syrup.

■ Cook the syrup until reduced and drizzle over the apples. Serve warm or chilled.

Serves 6

Note: *A nice side dish with ham or pork tenderloin.*

Cinnamon Roll-Ups

1	loaf soft white bread, crusts trimmed	3/4	cup (1 1/2 sticks) butter, melted
8	ounces cream cheese, softened		Cinnamon-sugar to taste

- Flatten each slice of bread with a rolling pin. Spread the cream cheese on one side of each slice of bread and roll to enclose the filling. Dip the rolls in the butter and coat with cinnamon and sugar. Cut each roll into four or five slices.

- Arrange the slices cut side down on a greased or parchment-lined baking sheet. Bake at 400 degrees for 5 minutes. Cool on a wire rack.

Serves 12

Note: *Do not allow soft bread to turn you off. These are really good. Freeze for future use, if desired.*

French Breakfast Muffins

1	cup sugar	2	teaspoons finely grated orange zest
2	teaspoons cinnamon		
1 1/2	cups all-purpose flour	1/3	cup shortening
1 1/2	teaspoons baking powder	1/2	cup sugar
1/2	teaspoon salt	1	egg
1/4	teaspoon mace	1/2	cup milk
4	ounces cream cheese, softened	1/2	cup (1 stick) butter, melted

- Mix 1 cup sugar and the cinnamon in a bowl. Combine the flour, baking powder, salt and mace in a bowl and mix well. Mix the cream cheese and orange zest in a bowl.

- Beat the shortening in a mixing bowl until creamy. Add 1/2 cup sugar and the egg and beat until blended. Add the flour mixture alternately with the milk, mixing just until combined after each addition.

- Fill lightly greased muffin cups one-third full, using half the batter. Layer each with 1 teaspoon of the cream cheese mixture and top with the remaining batter, filling the muffin cups two-thirds full.

- Bake at 350 degrees for 20 to 25 minutes or until golden brown. Remove the muffins from the pan immediately. Dip the tops in the butter and then in the cinnamon-sugar mixture. Serve warm.

Makes 2 dozen

Sweet Potato Muffins

1 1/2 cups all-purpose flour
2 teaspoons baking powder
1 teaspoon cinnamon
1/4 teaspoon salt
1/4 teaspoon nutmeg
1 1/4 cups sugar
1/2 cup (1 stick) butter, softened
2 eggs
1 1/4 cups canned sweet potatoes, mashed
1 cup milk
1/2 cup raisins, chopped
1/4 cup pecans or walnuts, chopped

- Mix the flour, baking powder, cinnamon, salt and nutmeg together in a bowl.
- Cream the sugar and butter in a mixing bowl, beating until light and fluffy. Add the eggs and beat until blended. Beat in the sweet potatoes.
- Add the flour mixture alternately with the milk, mixing just until combined after each addition. Do not overmix. Fold in the raisins and pecans.
- Fill twenty-four greased miniature muffin cups two-thirds full with the batter. Bake at 350 degrees for 20 minutes or until the muffins test done.
- Cool in the pan for 2 minutes and remove to a wire rack.

Makes 2 dozen

Carrot Pumpkin Muffins

1 1/2 cups whole wheat flour
1 1/2 teaspoons pumpkin pie spice
1 teaspoon baking soda
1 teaspoon baking powder
1 cup canned pumpkin
3/4 cup honey
1 egg, lightly beaten
2 tablespoons applesauce
1 tablespoon vegetable oil
1 cup shredded carrots

- Mix the whole wheat flour, pumpkin pie spice, baking soda and baking powder in a bowl.
- Whisk the pumpkin, honey, egg, applesauce and vegetable oil in a bowl until blended.
  Add the pumpkin mixture to the flour mixture and stir just until combined; do not overmix. Fold in the carrots.
- Spoon the batter into greased muffin cups.
- Bake at 350 degrees for 25 minutes or until a wooden pick inserted in the muffins comes out clean. Remove the muffins to a wire rack to cool.

Makes 1 dozen

Note: *These muffins can be served any time of the day but are delicious for breakfast.*

Ginger Muffins

4 cups all-purpose flour
2 teaspoons baking soda
1 teaspoon ginger
1/2 teaspoon salt
1/2 teaspoon cinnamon
1 1/4 cups shortening
1 cup sugar
4 eggs
1 cup cane syrup
1 cup well-shaken buttermilk

- Mix the flour, baking soda, ginger, salt and cinnamon together in a bowl.
- Cream the shortening and sugar in a mixing bowl, beating until light and fluffy. Add the eggs one at a time, mixing well after each addition. Stir in the syrup.
- Add the flour mixture alternately with the buttermilk to the creamed mixture, mixing just until combined after each addition. Chill, covered, in the refrigerator.
- Do not stir the batter. Fill greased muffin cups one-half full with the batter. Bake at 350 degrees for 15 to 18 minutes or until a wooden pick inserted in the centers comes out clean.
- Cool in the pan for 2 minutes and remove a wire rack.

Makes 4 dozen muffins

Note: The batter will keep for up to 6 weeks in an airtight container in the refrigerator. Muffins can be frozen in sealable plastic bags for up to 8 weeks. To serve, thaw at room temperature and reheat in a warm oven.

Pumpkin, Port and Ginger Bread

4¹/₂ cups all-purpose flour
1   tablespoon baking powder
2   teaspoons ginger
2   teaspoons cinnamon
1¹/₂ teaspoons salt
1   teaspoon baking soda
¹/₂ teaspoon nutmeg
¹/₂ teaspoon ground cloves
3   cups sugar

1   (13-ounce) can pumpkin
1   cup vegetable oil
1²/₃ cups port
6   eggs
1   cup chopped pecans, toasted
¹/₂ cup chopped crystallized
     ginger
¹/₂ cup golden raisins
     Orange Cream Cheese
     Frosting (*below*)

- Mix the flour, baking powder, ginger, cinnamon, salt, baking soda, nutmeg and cloves in a bowl.
- Combine the sugar, pumpkin, oil, port and eggs in a mixing bowl and beat just until blended. Do not overbeat. Add the flour mixture and stir until combined. Fold in the pecans, crystallized ginger and raisins.
- Spoon the batter into three greased and lightly floured 5×9-inch loaf pans.
- Bake at 350 degrees for 50 to 60 minutes or until the loaves test done.
- Cool in the pans for 15 minutes and remove to a wire rack to cool completely.
- Spread the Orange Cream Cheese Frosting on the cooled cakes.

Makes 3 loaves

Orange Cream Cheese Frosting

16   ounces cream cheese, softened
²/₃ cup confectioners' sugar
¹/₄ cup orange marmalade
2   tablespoons grated orange zest
2   tablespoons orange juice
     Pinch of salt

- Combine the cream cheese, confectioners' sugar, marmalade, orange zest, orange juice and salt in a mixing bowl.
- Beat until of a spreading consistency, adding additional orange juice to reach the desired consistency if necessary.

Makes about 2¹/₂ cups

Orange Bread

3/4 cup granulated sugar
1/2 cup chopped pecans
1 tablespoon grated orange zest
2 (10-count) cans refrigerator buttermilk biscuits
8 ounces cream cheese, cut into 20 cubes
1/2 cup (1 stick) butter, melted
1 cup sifted confectioners' sugar
2 tablespoons orange juice

- Mix the granulated sugar, pecans and orange zest in a bowl.

- Separate the biscuits into individual biscuits. Gently separate each biscuit into halves.

- Place one cream cheese cube between the biscuit halves and pinch the sides to seal. Dip in the butter and coat with the pecan mixture.

- Stand the biscuits on edge spacing evenly in a lightly greased 12-cup bundt pan. Sprinkle with the remaining pecan mixture.

- Bake at 350 degrees for 45 minutes or until golden brown. Invert onto a serving platter immediately.

- Mix the confectioners' sugar and orange juice in a bowl and drizzle over the warm bread. Serve immediately.

Serves 6

Note: Delicious cream cheese-filled sugar-crusted coffee cake. You may prepare in advance and reheat just before serving.

Cranberry Orange Bread

1/4 cup orange juice
2   tablespoons vegetable oil
2   cups all-purpose flour
1   cup sugar
11/2 teaspoons baking soda
1   teaspoon salt
     Grated zest of 1 orange
1   egg, beaten
1   cup chopped walnuts
1   cup chopped fresh cranberries

- Combine the orange juice and oil with enough water to measure 3/4 cup.
- Mix the flour, sugar, baking soda, salt and orange zest in a bowl. Add the orange juice mixture gradually, stirring constantly until combined. Stir in the egg and fold in the walnuts and cranberries.
- Spoon the batter into a greased 5×9-inch loaf pan and let stand for 20 minutes.
- Bake at 350 degrees for 1 hour. Cool in the pan for 10 minutes and remove to a wire rack to cool completely.

Makes 1 loaf

Note: If fresh cranberries are not available, rehydrate dried cranberries by soaking in orange juice.

Peanut Butter Bread

1½ cups sifted flour
1   cup sugar
1   tablespoon baking powder
½   teaspoon salt
¾   cup peanut butter
1   cup rolled oats
1   cup milk
2   eggs, beaten

- Mix the flour, sugar, baking powder and salt in a bowl. Cut in the peanut butter with a knife until crumbly. Add the oats, milk and eggs and mix well.
- Spoon the batter into a greased 5×9-inch loaf pan.
- Bake at 350 degrees for 1 hour. Cool in the pan for 10 minutes and remove to a wire rack to cool. Serve with butter and jam.
- The flavor of the bread is enhanced if allowed to stand for 8 to 10 hours or overnight before slicing.

Makes 1 loaf

Note: *This blue ribbon recipe can be made with smooth or crunchy peanut butter. Gives new meaning to "peanut butter and jelly."*

Sausage Breakfast Bread

1   cup raisins
3   cups all-purpose flour
1   teaspoon ginger
1   teaspoon baking powder
1   teaspoon pumpkin pie spice
1   teaspoon baking soda
1   cup cold strong coffee
1   pound bulk pork sausage
1 1/2 cups packed brown sugar
1 1/2 cups granulated sugar
2   eggs
1   cup chopped pecans or walnuts

- Simmer the raisins with a small amount of water in a saucepan for 4 to 5 minutes or until tender; drain.
- Sift the flour, ginger, baking powder and pumpkin pie spice into a bowl and mix well. Stir the baking soda into the coffee.
- Mix the sausage, brown sugar and granulated sugar in a mixing bowl. Beat in the eggs until combined. Add the flour mixture alternately with the coffee mixture, beating well after each addition. Stir in the raisins and pecans.
- Spoon the batter into a greased and floured 9-inch tube pan.
- Bake at 350 degrees for 1 1/2 hours or until a wooden pick inserted near the center comes out clean.

Serves 12

Note: This is a sensational breakfast bread and can be stored, wrapped in foil, in the refrigerator. It makes a welcome hostess gift.

Bourbon Slush

2   tea bags
1   cup hot water
3/4 cup sugar
3¹/2 cups water
1   cup bourbon
1   (6-ounce) can frozen orange juice concentrate
1   (6-ounce) can frozen lemonade concentrate

- Steep the tea bags in the hot water in a heatproof container for 5 minutes. Discard the tea bags.
- Add the sugar and stir until the sugar dissolves. Stir in 3^1/2 cups water, the bourbon, orange juice concentrate and lemonade concentrate.
- Freeze until slushy. Spoon into wine, liqueur or sherry glasses to serve.

Serves 8

Note: This will pull anyone out of a slump . . . a great pick-me-up. Keep on hand in the freezer for those unexpected guests.

Spiced Iced Tea

3   cups boiling water
5   cinnamon-apple flavor tea bags
9   cups water
2   cups unsweetened pineapple juice
1^1/2 cups sugar
1   (6-ounce) can frozen orange juice concentrate, thawed
1   (6-ounce) can frozen lemonade concentrate, thawed
    Lemon slices

- Pour the boiling water over the tea bags in a heatproof container. Steep, covered, for 5 minutes. Remove the tea bags, squeezing gently to release any tea.
- Stir in the water, pineapple juice, sugar, orange juice concentrate and lemonade concentrate. Chill, covered, in the refrigerator.
- Pour the tea over ice in glasses. Garnish each serving with a lemon slice.

Makes 1 gallon (16 cups)

Wedding Brunch

A great honor in a southeastern North Carolina wedding is to be able to host the wedding luncheon. We take great pride in our freshly polished silver and doily-lined plates. The daintiest dishes are shared at this elegant luncheon.

Candied Walnuts

Crab Canapés

Hearts of Palm Soup with Cumin Pepper Crisps

Bourbon Slush (as guests arrive)

Ham Soufflé with Mushroom Sauce

Confetti Grits

Hot Fruit

Peppered Pears

Gazpacho Aspic with Homemade Lemon Mayonnaise

Club Soda Biscuits

Carrot Pumpkin Muffins

Lemon Chiffon Ring with Fresh Fruit

Spiced Iced Tea

Champagne garnished with fresh sliced peaches

Mary Cassatt (American, 1844–1926)
Afternoon Tea Party, 1891
Drypoint and aquatint on paper
Gift of Therese Thorne McLane in honor of Samuel Hudson Hughes and Zelina Comegys Brunschwig

Desserts

The Cook's Canvas 2

Toasted Almond Pound Cake with Balsamic Strawberries

1 cup (2 sticks) butter, softened	1 cup almonds, toasted and ground
1 cup sugar	Balsamic Strawberries (*below*)
1/2 teaspoon almond extract	1 cup heavy whipping cream, whipped
4 eggs	
1 1/2 cups all-purpose flour	
1 teaspoon baking powder	

- Cream the butter, sugar and almond extract in a mixing bowl for 3 to 4 minutes or until light and fluffy. Scrape down the side of the bowl.
- Add the eggs one at a time, mixing well after each addition.
- Sift the flour and baking powder together. Add to the butter mixture and mix well. Fold in the almonds.
- Pour the batter into a buttered and floured 9×15-inch loaf pan.
- Bake at 350 degrees for 45 to 55 minutes or until a wooden pick inserted in the center comes out clean. Cool in the pan slightly. Remove to a cake plate.
- Slice the cake. Top each slice with Balsamic Strawberries and whipped cream.

Serves 8

Balsamic Strawberries

4 cups sliced strawberries (about 1 pound)
1/4 cup sugar
1 1/2 tablespoons balsamic vinegar

- Combine the strawberries, sugar and vinegar in a bowl and toss until coated.
- Let stand at room temperature for at least 1 hour.

Makes 4 cups

Note: *Serve the Balsamic Strawberries with mascarpone cheese or spooned over good-quality ice cream.*

Marmalade Cake

3/4 cup (1 1/2 sticks) butter, softened
1 cup sugar
1 tablespoon grated orange zest
1 tablespoon vanilla extract
3 eggs
1 cup good-quality bitter English orange marmalade
3 cups all-purpose flour
1 1/2 teaspoons baking soda
1 teaspoon salt
1/2 cup orange juice
1/2 cup evaporated milk
1 cup chopped pecans or walnuts
1/3 cup orange juice
1/3 cup sugar

■ Cream the butter and 1 cup sugar in a mixing bowl, beating until light and fluffy. Add the orange zest and vanilla and mix well.

■ Add the eggs one at a time, mixing well after each addition. Add the marmalade and mix well.

■ Sift the flour, baking soda and salt together.

■ Combine 1/2 cup orange juice and the evaporated milk and mix well.

■ Add the sifted ingredients to the butter mixture alternately with orange juice mixture, mixing well after each addition. Fold in the pecans.

■ Pour the batter into a buttered 10-inch tube pan.

■ Bake at 350 degrees for 55 to 60 minutes or until the cake tests done. Cool in the pan for 10 minutes. Remove to a cake plate.

■ Combine 1/3 cup orange juice and 1/3 cup sugar in a small saucepan and mix well. Cook over low heat until the sugar is completely dissolved, stirring constantly.

■ Pierce the top of the cake with a skewer, making many small holes. Spoon the glaze over the cake. Serve warm or at room temperature.

Serves 12 to 15

Note: This moist unglazed cake may be frozen for many months wrapped carefully in heavy duty foil. You may top this cake with purple and orange candied violas as the glaze is drying.

Fresh Pear Cake

4   cups (about 5) grated peeled and seeded pears
      (do not use Bosc pears)
2   cups sugar
1   cup pecans, chopped
1   cup vegetable oil
2   eggs, lightly beaten
1   teaspoon vanilla extract
3   cups all-purpose flour
2   teaspoons baking soda
1   teaspoon freshly grated nutmeg
$^1/_2$ teaspoon salt

- Combine the pears, sugar and pecans in a large bowl and toss until coated. Let stand for 1 hour.

- Stir in the vegetable oil, eggs and vanilla with a wooden spoon.

- Add the flour, baking soda, nutmeg and salt and mix well.

- Pour the batter into a buttered and floured large tube pan.

- Bake at 350 degrees for 1 hour and 15 minutes or until a wooden pick inserted in the center comes out clean. Do not overcook.

Serves 16

Note: This light cake is perfect to serve after a heavy meal. If the cake sticks to the pan, cover the bottom of the pan with a wet cloth for a few minutes.

Festive Pumpkin Roll

3   eggs
3/4 cup all-purpose flour
2   teaspoons cinnamon
1   teaspoon baking powder
1   teaspoon ginger
1/2 teaspoon nutmeg
1/2 teaspoon salt
1   cup granulated sugar

2/3 cup canned pumpkin or
     cooked fresh pumpkin
1   teaspoon fresh lemon juice
1   cup chopped pecans or
     walnuts
     Confectioners' sugar
     Cream Cheese Filling (*below*)

- Beat the eggs in a mixing bowl at high speed for 5 minutes or until light and fluffy.
- Combine the flour, cinnamon, baking powder, ginger, nutmeg and salt in a bowl and mix well. Fold into the eggs.
- Add the granulated sugar gradually, beating constantly. Stir in the pumpkin and lemon juice. Spread the batter evenly into a greased and floured 10×15-inch jelly roll pan. Sprinkle evenly with the pecans.
- Bake at 375 degrees for 15 minutes or until the cake tests done.
- Dust a clean kitchen towel with confectioners' sugar. Invert the cake onto the towel. Roll the warm cake in the towel from the short side or long side and place on a wire rack to cool.
- Unroll the cooled cake carefully and remove the towel. Spread the Cream Cheese Filling within 1 inch of the edge and reroll. Wrap in plastic wrap and then foil. Chill in the refrigerator until serving time. Slice with a serrated knife.

Serves 12

Cream Cheese Filling

6   ounces cream cheese, softened
4   teaspoons butter, softened
1   cup confectioners' sugar
1/2 teaspoon pure vanilla extract

- Cream the cream cheese and butter in a mixing bowl until light and fluffy.
- Add the confectioners' sugar and vanilla and blend until smooth. Chill, covered, until ready to use.

Makes about 1 1/2 cups

Almond Butter Cake

1 1/2 cups sugar
3/4 cup (1 1/2 sticks) butter, melted
2   eggs
1 1/2 cups all-purpose flour
1 1/2 teaspoons almond extract
1   teaspoon vanilla extract
1/2 teaspoon salt
3/4 cup (4 ounces) sliced almonds
1   tablespoon sugar
     Sliced fresh fruit (optional)

- Combine 1 1/2 cups sugar and the butter in a bowl and blend until smooth.
- Add the eggs and mix until creamy.
- Add the flour, almond extract, vanilla and salt and blend just until combined.
- Pour the batter into a 9-inch cake pan sprayed with nonstick cooking spray. Sprinkle evenly with the almonds and 1 tablespoon sugar.
- Bake at 350 degrees for 35 minutes or until light brown and a wooden pick inserted in the center comes out clean. Remove to a wire rack to cool for 30 minutes.
- Slice into wedges. Serve with sliced fresh fruit.

Serves 10

Note: This cake stays fresh for up to a week and freezes well.

Luscious Lava Cakes

3	ounces semisweet chocolate, finely chopped
1	ounce unsweetened chocolate, finely chopped
6	tablespoons unsalted butter, softened
6	tablespoons sugar
2	eggs
6	tablespoons all-purpose flour
1	tablespoon unsweetened baking cocoa
1/2	teaspoon baking powder
2	teaspoons unsalted butter, softened
	Whipped cream or ice cream
	Unsweetened baking cocoa

- Place the semisweet chocolate and unsweetened chocolate in the top of a double boiler over hot water. Cook until melted, stirring occasionally. Remove from the heat.

- Combine the melted chocolate, 6 tablespoons butter, and the sugar in a mixing bowl and blend until smooth.

- Add the eggs, flour, 1 tablespoon baking cocoa and the baking powder and beat for 5 minutes or until pale and thickened. Divide the batter into four ramekins buttered with 1/2 teaspoon butter each. Cover tightly with plastic wrap and freeze for 3 hours.

- Bake at 375 degrees for 10 to 11 minutes or until the edges are set and the centers are shiny. Invert onto dessert plates. Top with whipped cream and dust with baking cocoa. Serve immediately.

Serves 4

Note: An easy make-ahead dessert that will surely impress your guests.

Decadent Kahlúa Cake

1/2 cup sugar
1 (2-layer) package devil's food cake mix
3 eggs
3/4 cup brewed coffee
2/3 cup water
1/2 cup Kahlúa

1/3 cup bourbon
1/3 cup vegetable oil
2 teaspoons baking cocoa
Kahlúa Frosting (below)
Whipped cream
Maraschino cherries

■ Combine the sugar, cake mix, eggs, coffee, water, Kahlúa, bourbon, vegetable oil and cocoa in a mixing bowl and beat for 4 minutes. Pour the batter into a greased and floured tube pan. Bake at 350 degrees for 50 minutes.

■ Frost the cake with the Kahlúa Frosting. Slice the cake and place on dessert plates. Top each slice with whipped cream and a cherry.

Serves 8

Kahlúa Frosting

1/3 cup sugar
3 tablespoons evaporated milk
2 tablespoons butter

3/4 cup chocolate chips
1/4 cup Kahlúa

■ Combine the sugar, evaporated milk and butter in a saucepan. Bring to a boil, stirring frequently. Turn off the heat.

■ Stir in the chocolate chips and Kahlúa. Let stand until cool.

Makes about 1 cup

Note: Whipped cream is at stiff peak when the beater is lifted out and the whipped cream stands up straight. Soft peaks will hold shape but will have a curl.

Chocolate Amaretti Torte

1   cup (2 sticks) butter, softened
1   cup sugar
5   egg yolks
4   ounces amaretti (Italian macaroons)
1/2 cup all-purpose flour
2   ounces semisweet baking chocolate, grated
5   egg whites
     Confectioners' sugar

- Cream the butter and sugar in a mixing bowl, beating until light and fluffy.
- Add the egg yolks one at a time, mixing well after each addition.
- Process the amaretti in a food processor with a steel blade until ground to a powder consistency.
- Combine the ground amaretti and flour in a mixing bowl and mix well.
- Add the butter mixture gradually, mixing constantly until incorporated.
- Add the chocolate and mix well.
- Beat the egg whites in a separate mixing bowl until stiff peaks form.
- Stir 1/4 cup beaten egg whites into the batter. Fold in the remaining beaten egg whites. Spoon into a buttered and floured 10- or 12-inch springform pan.
- Bake at 350 degrees on the highest oven rack for 1 hour. Allow to cool before removing the side of the pan. Sprinkle with confectioners' sugar before serving.

Serves 8

Note: 4 ounces of amaretti are approximately 24 cookies.

Chocolate Raspberry Torte

1/2 cup blanched almonds, toasted
2 ounces unsweetened baking chocolate
2 tablespoons butter
2 eggs
1 cup sugar

1 tablespoon Framboise (raspberry-flavored liqueur)
3/4 cup all-purpose flour
1 teaspoon baking powder
1 teaspoon salt
1 cup raspberries
Raspberry Glaze and Chocolate Ganache (below)

- Process the almonds in a food processor until finely ground.

- Combine the chocolate and butter in the top of a double boiler over hot water. Cook until melted and smooth, stirring occasionally.

- Beat the eggs in a mixing bowl until pale yellow. Add the sugar gradually, beating constantly until thickened. Add the chocolate mixture and mix until smooth. Stir in the Framboise and almonds. Add the flour, baking powder and salt and mix just until combined. Fold in the raspberries. Pour into a buttered 9-inch springform pan.

- Bake at 350 degrees for 30 to 45 minutes or until the cake is firm and pulls away from the side of the pan. Let stand until cool.

- Invert the torte onto a wire rack placed on top of a rimmed baking sheet. Spread the Raspberry Glaze evenly over the top and side. Chill for 30 minutes.

- Pour the Chocolate Ganache over the torte, allowing the excess to drip down the side of the torte. Discard any excess collected in the rimmed baking sheet. Chill in the refrigerator until set.

Raspberry Glaze and Chocolate Ganache

2/3 cup seedless raspberry jam
1 tablespoon sugar
1/4 cup heavy cream

6 ounces semisweet chocolate, chopped

- To prepare the raspberry glaze, bring the jam and sugar to a boil in a saucepan.

- Cook for 3 minutes, stirring occasionally.

- To prepare the ganache, bring the cream to a boil in a saucepan.

- Remove from the heat and stir in the chocolate until melted. Let stand for 4 minutes.

Serves 8

Chocolate Bread Pudding with Whiskey Sauce

7   cups French bread,
    cut into cubes
3/4 cup (1¹/2 sticks) butter
2   cups whipping cream
1   cup milk

8   ounces bittersweet
    chocolate chopped
5   egg yolks, lightly beaten
2/3 cup packed brown sugar
1   teaspoon vanilla extract
    Whiskey Sauce (*below*)

- Sauté the bread in the butter in a skillet over medium heat until golden brown. Place in a greased 9×13-inch baking dish.

- Combine the cream and milk in a saucepan. Bring to a simmer over medium heat. Remove from the heat. Add the chocolate and whisk until melted and smooth.

- Whisk in the egg yolks, brown sugar and vanilla. Pour evenly over the bread, tossing to coat the bread well. Let stand for 30 minutes.

- Cover with foil and poke several holes in the foil.

- Place the baking dish in a larger baking pan. Add boiling water to the larger pan to a depth of 1¹/2 inches. Bake at 325 degrees for 1 hour and 45 minutes.

- Drizzle the Whiskey Sauce on top of the warm pudding or serve on the side.

Serves 8

Whiskey Sauce

1¹/2 cups milk
1   cup sugar
¹/2 cup (1 stick) butter

¹/4 cup water
3   tablespoons cornstarch
¹/2 cup bourbon whiskey

- Cook the milk, sugar and butter in a saucepan until heated through and the butter melts, stirring frequently.

- Combine the water and cornstarch in a small bowl and mix until the cornstarch is dissolved. Stir into the milk mixture.

- Stir in the whiskey and bring the mixture to a boil. Cook for 1 minute, stirring constantly. Remove from the heat.

Makes about 3 cups

Note: *At a party this dessert will disappear quickly.*

Pineapple Pudding

8   slices day-old bread
2   cups drained crushed pineapple
3/4 cup packed brown sugar
1/2 cup (1 stick) butter, melted
4   eggs, lightly beaten
2   cups heavy whipping cream
1   teaspoon crème de menthe, or to taste
    Sprigs of mint

- Cut the bread into 1-inch cubes.

- Combine the bread and pineapple in a bowl and mix well. Spread into a greased 1½-quart baking dish.

- Combine the brown sugar, butter and eggs in a bowl and mix well. Pour evenly over the bread mixture.

- Bake at 450 degrees for 30 to 40 minutes. Reduce the temperature to 350 degrees after 20 minutes of baking if the pudding is getting too brown.

- Combine the cream and crème de menthe in a mixing bowl and beat until stiff peaks form.

- Serve the pudding with the whipped cream on the side. Garnish with mint.

Serves 8

Lemon Chiffon Ring with Fresh Fruit

4	teaspoons unflavored gelatin	6	egg whites
1/2	cup cold water	1/3	cup sugar
2/3	cup sugar	1	cup seedless grapes
2/3	cup lemon juice	2	cups fresh strawberries
6	egg yolks	1	cup whipped cream
1/8	teaspoon salt		(optional)
2	teaspoons grated lemon zest		Mint leaves

- Sprinkle the gelatin over the cold water in a bowl. Let stand until softened.

- Combine 2/3 cup sugar and the lemon juice in a bowl and mix well.

- Beat the egg yolks and salt at high speed in a heatproof mixing bowl until pale yellow
  and thick.

- Add the lemon mixture to the egg yolk mixture gradually, beating constantly until blended.

- Place the bowl over hot water in a double boiler. Cook the mixture, stirring constantly, until thick enough to coat the back of a spoon. Remove from the heat.

- Add the gelatin and mix until dissolved. Stir in the lemon zest.

- Chill, covered, until the mixture begins to thicken.

- Beat the egg whites in a mixing bowl until soft peaks form. Add 1/3 cup sugar, 1 tablespoon at a time, beating well after each addition. Beat until stiff peaks form.

- Fold the egg white mixture into the gelatin mixture. Spoon into a large ring mold.

- Chill, covered, until firm.

- Invert onto a serving plate. Fill the center with the grapes and strawberries. Frost with whipped cream and garnish with mint leaves.

Serves 8

Lemon Mousse Cake

3	dozen ladyfingers	1	cup (2 sticks) cold butter
1	dozen coconut macaroons	1	cup whipping cream, whipped
2	cups water		
1	cup sugar	1/4	cup sugar
1/2	cup cornstarch		Colored sugar (optional)
1/2	cup fresh lemon juice	1	lemon, sliced (optional)
5	egg yolks		

■ Line the bottom of a 9×10-inch springform pan with waxed paper.

■ Arrange the ladyfingers upright around the edges of the pan, with the flat side facing in. Line the bottom of the pan with the macaroons.

■ Combine the water, 1 cup sugar, the cornstarch, lemon juice and egg yolks in a saucepan over medium heat and bring to a boil, stirring constantly. Cook for 1 minute or until thickened, stirring constantly. Remove from the heat.

■ Add the butter 1 tablespoon at a time, stirring after each addition until the butter is melted and blended.

■ Spoon the custard into the prepared pan, filling half the pan. Layer with half the remaining ladyfingers, half the remaining macaroons and the remaining custard. Top with the remaining ladyfingers and remaining macaroons.

■ Cover with a piece of waxed paper and seal tightly with plastic wrap. Chill in the refrigerator for 1 to 5 days.

■ Beat the cream and sugar in a mixing bowl until stiff peaks form. Spoon into a piping bag with a decorative nozzle.

■ Unmold the cake onto a cake plate and remove the side and bottom of the pan.

■ Decorate the cake with the whipped cream, piping rosettes between each ladyfinger on the side, over the top and around the top and bottom edges. Sprinkle with colored sugar and top with lemon slices.

Serves 10

Clemson Blue Cheesecake with Cranberry Compote

1½ cups graham cracker crumbs
⅓ cup butter, melted
22 ounces cream cheese, softened
¾ cup crumbled Clemson blue cheese
¾ cup plus 2 tablespoons sugar
3 tablespoons all-purpose flour

3 eggs
1 cup sour cream
2 teaspoons vanilla extract
Cranberry Compote (*below*)
Blue cheese crumbles
Sprig of mint

- Combine the graham cracker crumbs and butter in a bowl and mix well.
- Press over the bottom and 1 inch up the side of a 9-inch springform pan sprayed with nonstick cooking spray.
- Combine the cream cheese, ¾ cup blue cheese and the sugar in a bowl and beat until smooth.
- Add the flour and mix well.
- Add the eggs one at a time, mixing well after each addition.
- Add the sour cream and vanilla and blend until smooth. Pour over the crust.
- Bake at 300 degrees for 1 hour or until the cheesecake is firm. Do not overcook or the cheesecake will crack. Cool in the pan. Slice and place on dessert plates. Drizzle each slice with the warm Cranberry Compote. Garnish with blue cheese crumbles and mint.

Serves 10 to 12

Cranberry Compote

⅔ cup sugar
2 cups red wine
3 cups dried cranberries

- Combine the sugar and wine in a saucepan and bring to a boil. Reduce the heat and simmer for 3 to 5 minutes or until the sugar is dissolved, stirring often.
- Add the cranberries and cook for 5 to 7 minutes or until soft.

Makes 5 cups

Strawberry-Glazed Cheesecake

3/4 cup (3 ounces) walnuts
3/4 cup graham cracker crumbs
3 tablespoons butter, melted
32 ounces cream cheese, softened
4 eggs
1 1/4 cups sugar
1 tablespoon lemon juice
1 tablespoon vanilla extract
2 cups sour cream
1/4 cup sugar
1 teaspoon vanilla extract
1 quart strawberries, caps removed
12 ounces red raspberry jelly or jam
1 tablespoon cornstarch
1/4 cup water
1/4 cup Cointreau

- Pulse the walnuts in a food processor until chopped.

- Combine the walnuts, graham cracker crumbs and melted butter in a bowl and mix well. Press the walnut mixture over the bottom of a greased 9-inch springform pan.

- Beat the cream cheese in a mixing bowl until light and fluffy.

- Add the eggs, 1 1/4 cups sugar, the lemon juice and 1 tablespoon vanilla and beat until smooth and creamy. Pour over the prepared crust.

- Bake at 350 degrees for 1 hour or until firm. The top may turn light brown and crack. Let stand for 15 minutes.

- Combine the sour cream, 1/4 cup sugar and 1 teaspoon vanilla in a bowl and blend until smooth. Spread over the top of the cheesecake.

- Bake for 5 minutes; cool in the pan. Chill, covered, for 24 hours or for up to 3 days.

- Remove the side of the pan and place the cake on a cake plate. Cover the top of the cake with the strawberries, point end up.

- Combine the jelly and cornstarch in a small saucepan and mix well. Stir in the water and Cointreau. Cook over medium heat for 5 minutes or until bubbly, stirring occasionally. Let stand until cool.

- Drizzle the glaze evenly over the strawberries, coating the strawberries and dripping down the side of the cake.

- Chill in the refrigerator for 2 to 3 minutes or until the glaze is set.

Serves 10

Note: This rich velvety cheesecake makes a beautiful presentation.

Strawberry Ice Cream

> 2   cups strawberries
> 1   cup sugar
>   Juice of 1 lemon
> 1   cup whipping cream
> 2   cups milk

- Mash the strawberries in a large bowl. Add the sugar and lemon juice and mix well.
- Add the cream and milk and mix well. Pour the mixture into a shallow metal pan.
- Cover and freeze, stirring occasionally until set.

Serves 8

Baked Bananas

> 4   bananas
> 1/4   cup packed brown sugar
> 1/2   cup orange juice
> 1/4   teaspoon nutmeg
> 1/4   teaspoon cinnamon
> 1/2   to 3/4 cup rum
> 1   tablespoon butter

- Peel and cut the bananas lengthwise into halves. Arrange in a single layer in a baking dish.
- Combine the brown sugar, orange juice, nutmeg, cinnamon and rum in a saucepan. Cook until the sugar has dissolved and the mixture is smooth, stirring constantly.
- Drizzle evenly over the bananas. Dot with the butter.
- Bake at 450 degrees for 10 to 15 minutes, basting frequently with the syrup.
- Sprinkle with additional rum just before serving.

Serves 4

Note: For a variation of Bananas Foster, serve the baked bananas over vanilla ice cream. Drizzle with Praline Sauce (page 250) and sprinkle with Candied Walnuts (page 27).

Cranberry Rum Relish

5	whole navel oranges	1	tablespoon ginger
3	(12-ounce) packages fresh cranberries	1	tablespoon cinnamon
2	(15-ounce) packages golden raisins	1	tablespoon cloves
7	cups sugar		Rum to taste
1	cup distilled white vinegar		Ice cream or miniature phyllo pastry cups
			Brandied hard sauce

- Process the oranges in a food processor until finely chopped.

- Combine the oranges, cranberries, raisins, sugar, vinegar, ginger, cinnamon and cloves in a saucepan. Cook until the cranberries have popped open. Let stand until cool. Stir in rum.

- Spoon the relish into jars with tight-fitting lids. Chill in the refrigerator until ready to serve.

- Serve over ice cream or spoon into pastry cups and top with hard sauce.

Makes 9 pints

Note: Also serve this relish with meats and poultry. It is a welcome gift for family and friends during the holidays. If cranberries are out of season, dried cranberries may be used instead.

Praline Sauce

1	cup packed brown sugar	1	teaspoon vanilla extract
1/2	cup half-and-half	1	cup pecans
1/4	cup light corn syrup		Ice cream
2	tablespoons butter		

- Combine the brown sugar, half-and-half, corn syrup and butter in a saucepan. Cook over medium heat for 10 minutes or until thickened, stirring constantly.

- Remove from the heat and stir in the vanilla and pecans.

- Serve spooned over ice cream.

Makes 2 cups

Note: This sauce is especially delicious served over coffee ice cream.

Toffee Bar Trifle

1   (4-ounce) package vanilla instant pudding mix
3   cups half-and-half
1/2   cup Kahlúa or amaretto
2   teaspoons instant coffee granules
2   cups heavy whipping cream
1/4   cup sugar
1   tablespoon vanilla extract
1   angel food cake, torn into bite-sized pieces
8   ounces toffee candy bars, chopped

■ Prepare the pudding according to the package directions using the half-and-half instead of milk.

■ Stir in the Kahlúa or amaretto.

■ Chill, covered, in the refrigerator until partially set.

■ Sprinkle the instant coffee over the cream in a mixing bowl. Chill for 1 to 2 minutes. Beat until soft peaks form. Add the sugar and vanilla gradually and beat until stiff peaks form.

■ Spread a small amount of the pudding mixture in the bottom of a trifle dish. Layer the angel food cake, remaining pudding mixture, whipped cream and toffee candy bars one-half at a time. Chill, covered, in the refrigerator until serving time.

Serves 8

Note: *This dessert is even better served the second day.*

Banana Pudding Extravaganza

2 cups all-purpose flour
1 cup chopped pecans
1 cup (2 sticks) butter, melted
1^1/4 cups whipping cream
4 ounces cream cheese, softened
^{1}/2 cup sifted confectioners' sugar
2 (3-ounce) packages vanilla instant pudding mix
2^1/2 cups milk
2 bananas
1 cup heavy whipping cream
^{1}/2 cup chopped pecans, toasted
^{1}/2 cup flaked coconut, toasted

- Combine the flour, 1 cup pecans and the butter in a bowl and mix well. Press over the bottom of a 9×13-inch baking dish.

- Bake at 350 degrees on a rack in the lower third of the oven for 25 minutes or until light brown. Let stand until cool.

- Combine 1^1/4 cups cream, the cream cheese and confectioners' sugar in a mixing bowl and mix well. Spread evenly over the crust. Chill, covered, in the refrigerator.

- Combine the pudding mix and milk in a bowl and whisk until thickened. Spread evenly over the cream cheese layer. Chill, covered, in the refrigerator.

- Slice the banana into thin rounds about the width of a coin and arrange in a single layer over the pudding.

- Whip 1 cup cream in a bowl until stiff peaks form. Fold in ^{1}/2 cup toasted pecans and spread evenly over the bananas. Sprinkle with the coconut. Chill, covered, until serving time.

Serves 10

Date and Sesame Won Tons

1/4 cup sesame seeds	1 tablespoon butter, softened
1/4 cup packed brown sugar	Won ton wrappers
1/2 cup finely chopped	Peanut oil for frying
pitted dates	Confectioners' sugar

■ Bake the sesame seeds at 200 degrees on a baking sheet until golden brown. Pulse in a food processor with a steel blade until ground.

■ Mix the ground sesame seeds, brown sugar, dates and butter in a bowl. Spoon about 1 teaspoon of the mixture onto each won ton wrapper. Fold the wrapper to enclose the date mixture and seal the edges with water. May be frozen until ready to fry.

■ Deep-fry the won tons in peanut oil in a wok for 1 minute or until golden brown; drain. Dust with confectioners' sugar.

Makes 3 dozen

Maple Spice Cookies

2 cups all-purpose flour	1/4 cup granulated sugar
1 1/4 teaspoons ginger	1/4 cup maple syrup
1/2 teaspoon cinnamon	1/4 cup unsulphured molasses
1/2 teaspoon allspice	1 egg
1/4 teaspoon baking soda	1/2 cup raisins
1/4 teaspoon salt	1/2 cup chopped mixed dried
1 cup (2 sticks) butter, softened	fruit or dried cranberries
1/2 cup packed brown sugar	

■ Sift the flour, ginger, cinnamon, allspice, baking soda and salt into a bowl.

■ Cream the butter, brown sugar and granulated sugar in a mixing bowl, beating until light and fluffy. Add the maple syrup, molasses and egg and beat until combined.

■ Stir in the sifted dry ingredients with a wooden spoon. Stir in the raisins and dried fruit. Drop by tablespoonfuls onto a cookie sheet.

■ Bake at 375 degrees for 12 minutes or until set. Cool on a wire rack.

Makes 4 dozen

Variation: This recipe can adapt to your party theme. Use exotic fruit for an island flair, berries for a garden party or cranberries for the holidays.

Crispy Oatmeal Cookies

1 cup (2 sticks) butter, softened
1 cup granulated sugar
1 cup packed brown sugar
1 egg
1 cup vegetable oil
1 teaspoon vanilla extract
3 1/2 cups all-purpose flour
1 teaspoon baking soda
1/2 teaspoon salt
1 cup rolled oats
1 cup crushed cornflakes
1/2 cup shredded coconut
1/2 chopped pecans or walnuts

- Cream the butter in a mixing bowl until fluffy. Add the granulated sugar and brown sugar gradually, beating constantly until light and fluffy. Add the egg and mix well. Stir in the vegetable oil and vanilla. Add a mixture of the flour, baking soda and salt and mix well. Stir in the oats, cereal, coconut and pecans.

- Shape the dough into 1-inch balls and place 2 inches apart on a cookie sheet; flatten with a fork. Bake at 325 degrees for 15 minutes. Cool slightly on the cookie sheet. Remove to a wire rack to cool completely.

Makes 6 dozen

Almond Macaroons

3/4 cup blanched almonds, or
  1 cup slivered blanched
  almonds
1/2 cup sugar
1 tablespoon amaretto (optional)
1/4 teaspoon almond extract
1/4 teaspoon salt
2 egg whites
1/3 cup slivered almonds

- Line a cookie sheet with buttered baking parchment.

- Combine 3/4 cup almonds, the sugar, amaretto, almond extract and salt in a food processor with a steel blade. Process until finely ground. Beat the egg whites in a mixing bowl until foamy and soft peaks form. Fold in the almond mixture gently.

- Spoon in 1-inch mounds about 2 inches apart onto the prepared cookie sheet. Sprinkle with 1/3 cup almonds. Bake at 300 degrees for 15 to 20 minutes or until the edges brown. Cool on the cookie sheet. Store in an airtight container for up to 2 weeks.

Makes 2 dozen

Note: *These cookies don't turn out well if made on a rainy day.*

Orange Chocolate Chip Cookies

1   cup (2 sticks) butter, softened
2/3 cup packed light brown sugar
2/3 cup granulated sugar
1   egg
1   teaspoon vanilla extract
13/4 cups all-purpose flour
1/2 teaspoon baking soda
1/4 teaspoon salt
6   ounces good-quality bittersweet chocolate, broken into pieces
3   ounces good-quality milk chocolate, broken into pieces
11/2 cups old-fashioned rolled oats
1   cup sweetened grated coconut
1   cup coarsely chopped pecans
    Grated zest of 3 oranges

- Cream the butter, brown sugar and granulated sugar in a mixing bowl, beating until light and fluffy.

- Add the egg and vanilla and mix well.

- Stir in the flour, baking soda and salt with a wooden spoon.

- Fold in the bittersweet chocolate, milk chocolate, oats, coconut, pecans and orange zest.

- Drop by rounded tablespoonfuls 2 inches apart on a lightly greased cookie sheet.

- Bake at 375 degrees for 12 minutes or until golden brown. Cool on a wire rack.

Makes 4 dozen

Note: The orange zest makes this an exciting variation on a classic cookie recipe.

Chocolate Layer Bars

2 cups (12 ounces) semisweet chocolate chips
8 ounces cream cheese
2/3 cup evaporated milk
1 cup chopped walnuts
1/2 teaspoon almond extract
3 cups all-purpose flour

1 1/2 cups sugar
1 cup (2 sticks) butter, softened
2 eggs
1 teaspoon baking powder
1/2 teaspoon almond extract
1/2 teaspoon salt

■ Combine the chocolate, cream cheese and evaporated milk in a saucepan. Cook over low heat until the chocolate is melted and the mixture is smooth, stirring constantly. Remove from the heat. Stir in the walnuts and 1/2 teaspoon almond extract.

■ Combine the flour, sugar, butter, eggs, baking powder, 1/2 teaspoon almond extract and salt in a mixing bowl. Mix until the mixture resembles coarse crumbs. Press half the dough into a greased 13×19-inch rimmed baking pan. Spread the chocolate mixture evenly on top. Sprinkle the remaining dough on top.

■ Bake at 375 degrees for 40 minutes or until golden brown. Let stand until cool and cut into bars.

Makes 3 dozen

Chocolate Bites

1 (1-pound) package confectioners' sugar
2 cups peanut butter
1 cup unsalted peanuts
3/4 cup packed brown sugar

1/2 cup (1 stick) butter, softened
2 cups (12 ounces) semisweet chocolate chips
1 tablespoon butter

■ Combine the confectioners' sugar, peanut butter, peanuts, brown sugar and 1/2 cup butter in a bowl and mix well. Press into a 10×15-inch rimmed baking pan. Flatten the top with a rolling pin.

■ Microwave the chocolate chips and 1 tablespoon butter in a microwave-safe bowl on High at 30-second intervals until melted and smooth, stirring after each interval.

■ Spread the chocolate mixture evenly over the peanut butter layer. Cut into bite-size pieces. Chill for 15 to 20 minutes or until firm. Remove from the pan and serve.

Makes 2 dozen

Pecan Clusters

4   cups large pecan pieces
1/4 cup (1/2 stick) butter, melted
     Dash of salt
1   pound good-quality white chocolate

- Combine the pecans with the butter and salt in a bowl and toss until coated. Spread evenly onto a baking sheet.
- Bake at 350 degrees for 10 to 12 minutes or until golden brown, stirring three or four times.
- Place the white chocolate in a microwave-safe bowl. Microwave on High at 30-second intervals until melted and smooth, stirring after each interval. Stir in the pecans.
- Drop by spoonfuls onto waxed paper and let stand until cool. Store in candy tins.

Makes 40

Brown Sugar Chess Pie

1   unbaked (9-inch) pie shell
2   cups packed brown sugar
1 1/2 teaspoons cornstarch
4   eggs

3   tablespoons whipping cream
1   teaspoon lemon juice
2   teaspoons vanilla extract
1/3   cup butter, melted and cooled

- Prick the bottom of the pie shell with a fork. Partially bake the pie shell according to the package directions.
- Combine the brown sugar and cornstarch in a bowl and mix well, pressing out any lumps.
- Add the eggs one at a time, mixing well after each addition.
- Stir in the cream, lemon juice and vanilla.
- Add the butter and mix well. Pour the filling into the pie shell.
- Bake at 325 degrees for 50 to 60 minutes or until puffed and brown. Let stand until cool. Serve at room temperature.

Serves 8

Note: To soften lumpy brown sugar, combine the brown sugar and a slice of apple in a microwave-safe bowl. Microwave for 15 seconds or until soft.

Peanut Butter Pie

1   cup graham cracker crumbs
3¹/2 tablespoons sugar
3   tablespoons all-purpose flour
3   tablespoons baking cocoa
     Pinch of cinnamon
3   tablespoons butter, melted
8   ounces cream cheese, softened
1   cup crunchy peanut butter
1   cup sugar
2   tablespoons butter, melted
1   cup heavy cream
1¹/2 teaspoons vanilla extract
3   ounces semisweet chocolate
1¹/2 tablespoons brewed coffee
¹/4 cup chopped peanuts

- Combine the graham cracker crumbs, 3¹/2 tablespoons sugar, the flour, baking cocoa and cinnamon in a bowl and mix well. Stir in 3 tablespoons melted butter.
- Press the graham cracker mixture over the bottom of a 9-inch pie plate; chill.
- Combine the cream cheese, peanut butter, 1 cup sugar and 2 tablespoons melted butter in a mixing bowl and beat until light and fluffy.
- Stir in the cream and vanilla. Pour into the chilled pie crust. Chill, covered, for 7 to 10 hours.
- Melt the chocolate in a saucepan over low heat, stirring constantly. Remove from the heat and stir in the coffee. Let stand until slightly cool.
- Spread evenly over the peanut butter layer and sprinkle with the chopped peanuts. Chill, covered, until serving time.

Serves 8

Note: *This pie may be frozen.*

Luscious Lemon Pie

1   unbaked No-Roll Pie Pastry shell (*below*)
3   eggs, lightly beaten
1   cup sugar
1/4   cup lemon juice
3   tablespoons instant flour
3/4   teaspoon baking powder
1/2   teaspoon lemon extract
     Unsweetened whipped cream

- Bake the pie shell at 400 degrees for 5 minutes or until partially baked. Remove from the oven. Reduce the oven temperature to 350 degrees.
- Combine the eggs, sugar, lemon juice, flour, baking powder and lemon extract in a bowl and mix until smooth. Pour into the No-Roll Pie shell.
- Bake for 20 to 25 minutes or until the center is almost set.
- Serve with whipped cream.

Serves 6 to 8

No-Roll Pie Pastry

1 1/2 cups all-purpose flour
1 1/2 teaspoons sugar
1   teaspoon salt
1/2   cup shortening
2   tablespoons cold milk

- Combine the flour, sugar and salt in a 9-inch pie plate and mix well.
- Beat the shortening and milk in a bowl with a fork until combined. Stir into the flour mixture and mix well.
- Press into the pie plate by hand. Prick the bottom and side with a fork.
- Bake at 400 degrees for 12 to 15 minutes when a pie recipe calls for a baked pie crust.

Makes one 9-inch pie shell

Note: Picking "I love you" on the bottom of the pastry shell before baking is a special southern tradition. For a 2-crust pie, double the recipe, divide in half and roll out between sheets of waxed paper.

Coconut Macaroon Pie

1/2 cup chopped pecans
1   unbaked (9-inch) pie shell
1 1/2 cups shredded coconut
1 1/2 cups sugar
1/2 cup water
1/2 cup (1 stick) butter, melted
1/4 cup all-purpose flour
2   eggs, lightly beaten
1/8 teaspoon salt

- Sprinkle the pecans evenly in the bottom of the pie shell.
- Combine the coconut, sugar, water, butter, flour, eggs and salt in a bowl and mix well. Pour evenly over the pecans. Do not stir.
- Bake at 325 degrees for 45 minutes or until golden brown.

Serves 8

Caribbean Fudge Pie

2   cups (12 ounces) chocolate chips
1   cup chopped pecans
3/4 cup sugar
1/4 cup (1/2 stick) butter, softened
3   eggs
2   teaspoons brewed coffee
1   teaspoon Tia Maria
1   uncooked (9-inch) pie shell (optional)

- Melt the chocolate chips in a saucepan over low heat, stirring constantly. Remove from the heat.
- Stir in the pecans, sugar, butter, eggs, coffee and Tia Maria. Pour into a pie shell or an unlined pie plate.
- Bake at 350 degrees for 25 minutes or until the pie tests done.

Serves 8

Holiday Dessert Party

As Southerners, we always add a pinch of sugar to each recipe. A great entertaining idea is to host an after-performance dessert party. Rave reviews always accompany this evening.

Sweet Almond Cheese Delight with ginger thins
Apple Curry Spread
Toffee Bar Trifle
Strawberry-Glazed Cheesecake
Decadent Kahlúa Cake
Chocolate Raspberry Torte
Fresh Pear Cake
Maple Spice Cookies
Pecan Clusters
Almond Macaroons

Champagne
Port
Coffee and liqueurs

Champagne Flute Sponsors

C. Edward Alexander

Anonymous

Ben Barker

Fred and Ellen Barnette

Betsy Bede

Thomas Behm

Mary Boylan

Ralph and Pam Bradley

Ruth M. Brown

Clay Brumbaugh

Caroline K. Butts

Nan Cameron

Nadia Coble

Suzanne and Bill Coleman

Deborah Collins

Melissa Ann Corbett

Phyllis Covell

Hope Cusick

Fred Davenport Jr.

Susan Dillard

Debbie Elliott

Farmer's Supply

Julie E. Fisher

R. V. Fulk Jr.

Margaret Gerlach

Ralph and Theresa Gevinson

Hilda Godwin

Connie Grine

Cathy Hargett

Susan Mixon Harrell

Stephanie Hendrickson

Aggie Henriksen

Melissa Herzog

Diana Holdridge

Intracoastal Realty Corporation

Annie Gray Johnston

Kathryn K. Johnston

Brent and Jennifer Kitchens

Linda Lavin

Martha Best Lawson

Rebecca Laymon

Jane P. Lewallen

Elizabeth L. Lowe

Katherine Marapese

Jacqueline Margoles

Shannon C. Maus

Anna Maynard

Rebecca C. McGowan

Kyle McIntyre

Richard Myracle

Betty Oliver

Margaret Palmer

Walter Pancoe

Sarah Parsley

Beth Quinn

Allison Rankin

Ralph Robins

Jean Rosenberg

Doris Ruffner

Carl K. Rust II

Amy Sanders

Anne Schaeffer

Mary Schumacher

Carolyn Simmons

Teresa Snyder

Betty Tinsley

Kelly Tinsley

Les and Ann Turlington

Tom and Susette van Arsdale

Kay Warner

Elaine Werner

Mat and Pat White

Kenneth Whipkey

Mary Whitehurst

Helene Winograd

Lyndia Wright

A gift from the docents in memory
of Dan Friedenreich

Special Thank You

Carriage House Florist

Dragonflies

Sweet and Savory

Sysco Foods of Raleigh

Donald Barickman

Mebane Boyd

Anne Brennan

C. Reynolds Brown

Debbi Causey

Sara Foster

Hilda Godwin

Roberta Hawkins

Pam Jobin

Amy Kilgore

Lynn Lowder

Erin Ottolini

Ben Parsley

Holly Tripman

Tom van Arsdale

Deborah Velders

Kenda Walters

Volunteers

Dot Addison
Gloria Amstutz
Gaye Andersen
Nancy Andre
Leilani Andrews
Sally Archer
Anna Averitt
Dors Ayers
John Balderson
Keith Ball
Mary Beth Bankson
Don Barickman
Joyce Barickman
Jim and Rosalind Barker
Boca Bay
Anne Beatty
Darrell Beauchaines
Betsy Bede
Layne Bede
Jayme Bednarczyk
Dorothy Berube
Lelia Birrell
Helen Bolles
Lynne Boney
Joan Boyd
Mary Boylan
Pam Bradley
Pam Brennan
Kay Britto
Jane Broder
Ruth Brown
Hannah Brownlow
Russ Bryan
Margaret Burdick
Susan Butler
Caroline Butts
Ruth Bynum
Betty Cameron

Mary Jo Cameron
Nan Cameron
Susan Carter
Becky Cary
Beth Cherry
Mary Coble
Nadia Coble
Ellen Coffey
Suzanne Coleman
Ceceila Corbett
Diana Corbett
Pat Coughlin
Phyllis Covell
Sandra Criner
Hope Cusick
Tahlia Davis
Elizabeth Deckworth
Elisabeth Dill
Hilda Dill
Margaret Dill
Susan Dillard
Anne Dols
Jane Donnelly
Cornelia Doss
Randi Duch
Mary Dunlap
Linda Easterlin
Delonna Echols
Carolyn Evans
Mary Lou Fedick
Louise Fenstermacher
Audrey Fetterman
Carole Fine
Katherine Fitzpatrick
Deborah Flora
Kate Fox
Dan and Judy
   Friedenreich

Betty Gaffney
Marge Gerlach
Polly Gibson
Hilda Godwin
Ralph and Hilda
   Godwin
Jimmie and Claudette
   Goetze
Katherine Goldberg
Jackie Gooch
Linda Grice
Connie Grine
Robin Hackney
Mary Haney
Christa Hare
Cathy Hargett
Patsy Harley
Patsy Moore Harley
Tony Harrington
Anne Haughn
Care Heeks
Gail Henderson
Stephanie Hendrickson
Aggie Henriksen
Ann Hertzler
Marian Hills
Lib Hobson
Mary Stewart Hood
Nate Hoffman
Linda Hundley
Alice Hunt
Jimmy and Carol
   Hunt
Harriet Iiames
Martha Jenkins
Annie Gray Johnston
Ruth Jordan
Jeanne Kendig

Rebekah King
Tiffany Kitchen
Brent and Jennifer
	Kitchens
Alex and Wilma
	Kuzmuk
Laura Labant
Linda Lavin
Martha Best Lawson
Melissa Leach
Terri Lensch
Laura Leonard
Kristine Lewis
Betsy Litwiler
Anne Livingston
Patrick Livingston
Trish Looney
Howard and Leli
	Loving
Lynn Lowder
Betty Lowe
Sarah Lowe
Kathy Lubbers
Jinger Lyon
Jayme Malta
Stephanie Mannen
Katherine Marapese
Pat Marriott
Joy Marshall
Jane Martin
Anna Maynard
Frances McMillan
Cindi McQuire
Gloria Meder
Carolyn Medley
Carol Milne
Alice Mintz
Shirley Morrow

Frankie Moulton
Charlotte Murchison
Leigh Murray
Player Murray
Jennifer Nance
Arlene Nazario
Lil Newton
Dean Ornish
Erin Ottolini
Lou Overman
Margaret Palmer
Patti Pancoe
Tiffani Pearson
Mary-Emily Pitt
Darlene Powell
Lucy Prell
Lisa Purdom
Linda Pyle
Joy Price
Margaret Pulmer
Betty and Gene
	Purcell
Pat Rathburn
Cindy Redfield
Henry Rehder
Phiney Rhinehart
Ann Richardson
Ann Robins
Margaret Robinson
Ann Rorick
Doris Ruffner
Polly Rust
Swanna Saltiel
Anne Schaeffer
Mary Schumacher
Carolyn Simmons
Emily and David Sloan
Dixey Smith

Anne Squire
Marty Stanfield
Jane Stephens
Eryn Stevens
Will Stevens
Anna Stone
Aglaea Stoycos
Jane Gray Suggs
Jane Sullivan
Katharine Sullivan
Sara Switzer
Suzanne Thatcher
Susan Thompson
Nancy Tillet
Gale Tolan
Karen Traina
Anne Turlington
Carol Vanderkieft
Martha C. Vann
Melinda Walker
Andrea Wallace
Allison Ward
Robin Ward
Dottie Werk
Elaine Werner
Gloria Werner
Mary Grace White
Mearlene White
Polly White
Kim Whitfield
Helene Winograd
Pat Winston
Lyndia Wright
Wrightsville Beach
	Magazine
Diane Wrzosek

Index

Index   267

Photography Information

Cover and Endsheet: Claude Howell (American, 1915–1997), *Beach Cottage,* 1981, oil on canvas. Gift of the friends of Claude Howell © by Claude Howell Estate/Cameron Art Museum. Photograph © 2007 by Cameron Art Museum. Page 10: Gwathmey Siegel & Associates Architects LLC, New York, NY, Detail of Cameron Art Museum. Photograph © by Brownie Harris. Page 44: Elisabeth Chant (English, 1865–1947), *Compositions: Pre-Gothic Days in Devon,* n.d., watercolor on paper. Gift of Henry MacMillian © by Elisabeth Chant Estate. Photograph © 2006 by Cameron Art Museum. Page 78: Utagawa Hiroshige (Japanese, 1797–1885), *Station 3 Kawasaki (From the Fifty-Three Stations of the Tōkaidō),* c.1855, woodblock print, Publisher: Tsutaya, Format: oban tateye. Gift of Dr. Isabel Bittinger. Photograph © 2006 by Cameron Art Museum. Page 112: Attributed to Caroline Von Glahn (American, 1843–1903), Untitled *(River and Millhouse),* n.d., pastel on paper. Gift of Katherine Von Glahn. Photograph © 2006 by Cameron Art Museum. Page 146: Elliot Daingerfield (American, 1859–1932), *Lotus Land,* c. 1920, oil on canvas. Purchased with funds from the Jessie N. Howell Memorial North Carolina Acquisitions Fund, Takeda Chemical and Tabitha McEachern. Photograph © 2007 by Cameron Art Museum. Page 164: Unknown (American, mid-nineteenth century), Detail of slave-made quilt, Tulip design, c.1850, cotton pieced quilt with double row stitching. Gift of Mildred and James Guthrie. Photograph © 2007 by Cameron Art Museum. Page 198: Mark Hewitt (English, 1955), *Yellow Dog,* 2001, wood fired salt glazed stoneware, alkaline glaze with blue-glass on shoulders. Purchased from the artist with funds from the Claude Howell Endowment for the Purchase of North Carolina Art © by Mark Hewitt. Photograph © by Jackson Smith. Page 232: Mary Cassatt (American, 1844–1926), *Afternoon Tea Party,* 1891, drypoint and aquatint on paper. Gift of Therese Thorne McLane in honor of Samuel Hudson Hughes and Zelina Comegys Brunschwig. Photograph © 2007 by Cameron Art Museum.

Order Information

Louise Wells Cameron Art Museum
3201 South 17th Street
Wilmington, North Carolina 28412
910.395.5999
www.cameronartmuseum.com